Turkish Recipes

A Turkish Cookbook with Easy Turkish Recipes

By
BookSumo Press
All rights reserved

Published by
http://www.booksumo.com

ENJOY THE RECIPES?

KEEP ON COOKING WITH 6 MORE FREE COOKBOOKS!

Visit our website and simply enter your email address to join the club and receive your 6 cookbooks.

http://booksumo.com/magnet

https://www.instagram.com/booksumopress/

https://www.facebook.com/booksumo/

LEGAL NOTES

All Rights Reserved. No Part Of This Book May Be Reproduced Or Transmitted In Any Form Or By Any Means. Photocopying, Posting Online, And / Or Digital Copying Is Strictly Prohibited Unless Written Permission Is Granted By The Book's Publishing Company. Limited Use Of The Book's Text Is Permitted For Use In Reviews Written For The Public.

Table of Contents

Chicken Kofte Bites 9

Turkish Mozzarella Casserole 10

Allspice Sweet Quinces Stew 11

Chicken Taro Stew 12

Turkish Breakfast 13

Lamb Stew with Turkish Baharat 14

Quick Beef Lunch Skillet 15

Cheese and Lamb Stuffed Pastry 16

Greek Style Feta Salad 18

Warm Leeks Salad 19

Saucy Rice Casserole 20

Turkish Ratatouille 21

Vanilla Chicken Pudding 22

Turkish Ratatouille 23

Zesty Carrot Sauté 24

Hot and Sweet Tomato Spread 25

Refreshing Watermelon Salad 26

Cheesy Eggplant Stuffed Pasties 27

Tagine Style Lamb Stew 28

Turkish Style Nuts Pilaf 29

Turkish Dill Patties 30

Chili Pea Soup 31

Turkish Pumpkin Candy 32

Saucy Eggplant Casserole 33

Easy Peasy Chickpea Falafels 34

Chicken Flavored Leeks Stew 35

Sesame Bread Wheels 36

Creamy Nectarine Chocolate Parfait 37

Bell Marinated Lamb Kebab 38

Walnut Egg Noodles Salad 39

Feta Fritters with Creamy Cucumber Sauce 40

Warm Veggies and Butter Beans Stew 41

Turkish Vanilla Cake 42

Ajvar Chicken Stew 43

Spicy Chicken Kabobs with Pomegranate Relish 44

Double Stuffed Eggplants 45

Saffron Rice Kebab 46

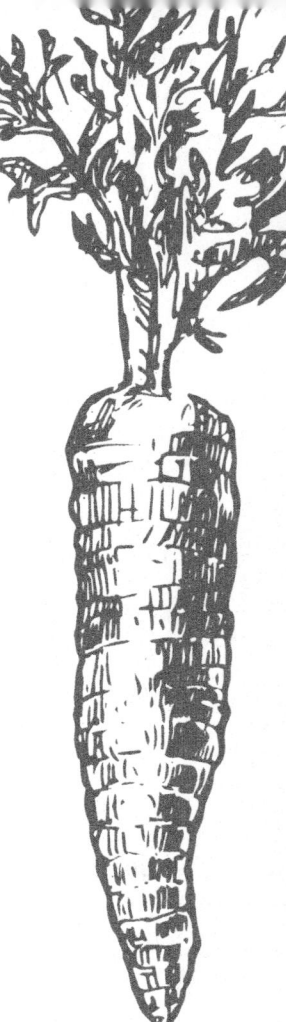

Hot Molasses Dip 47

Tofu Dessert Salad 48

Sultan's Delight Stew 49

Turkish Fish Stew 50

Haydari: (A Turkish Yogurt Dip) 51

Tava I: (A Turkish Stew) 52

Dondurma: (Turkish Ice Cream) 53

Breakfast Eggs in Turkey 54

Turkish Soup of Red Lentils 55

Classical Turkish Greens 56

Manti: (Turkish Ravioli) 57

Turkish Cookies 58

A Turkish Inspired Ceviche 59

Kisir: (A Turkish Bulgur and Vegetable Salad) 60

Classical Bulgur 61

Tava II: (Turkish Stew) 62

Iskender Kebabs 63

Moussaka: (Potato Casserole from the Ottoman Empire) 64

Dukkah: (Levantine Spice Mix) 65

Classical Turkish Chevre 66

Dukkah: (Levantine Spice Mix) 67

Dolmas: (Stuffed Grape Leaves) 68

Mediterranean Kofta 69

Hot Yogurt Chicken Thighs 70

Saucy Turkish Burger Meatloaf 71

Flaming Turkish Yogurt and Chicken Kebabs 72

Chicken Pilaf 73

Minty Potato Salad 74

Turkish Cheesy Spinach Pizza 75

Cherry Saucy Lamb Kabobs with Cucumber Salad 76

Saucy Greens Potato Salad 77

Spiced-Up Lamb Stew 78

Baharat Spice Mix at Home 79

Minty Feta and Courgette Patties 80

Hot Lamb Kabobs with Bloody Mary Hummus 81

Minty Beef Sandwiches 82

Mediterranean Omelets 83

Feta Chicken Pizza 84

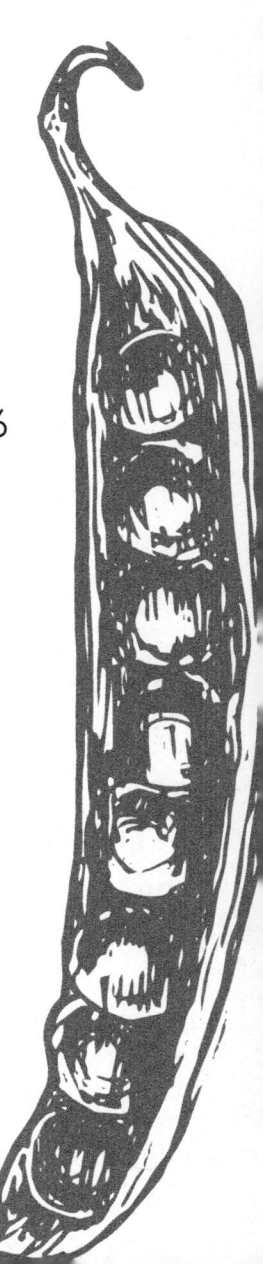

Karniyarik: (Turkish Eggplants) 85

Tzatziki Steak Kabobs 86

Turkish Small Burgers 87

Minty Lamb Pizza with Garlic Cream Sauce 88

Golden Shrimp Bites 90

Greek Style Turkish Chicken Kabobs 91

Tilapia and Couscous Stew 92

Yogurt Sauce with Poached Eggs Breakfast 93

Cheesy Chicken Casserole 94

Warm Lentil Salad with Yogurt Sauce 95

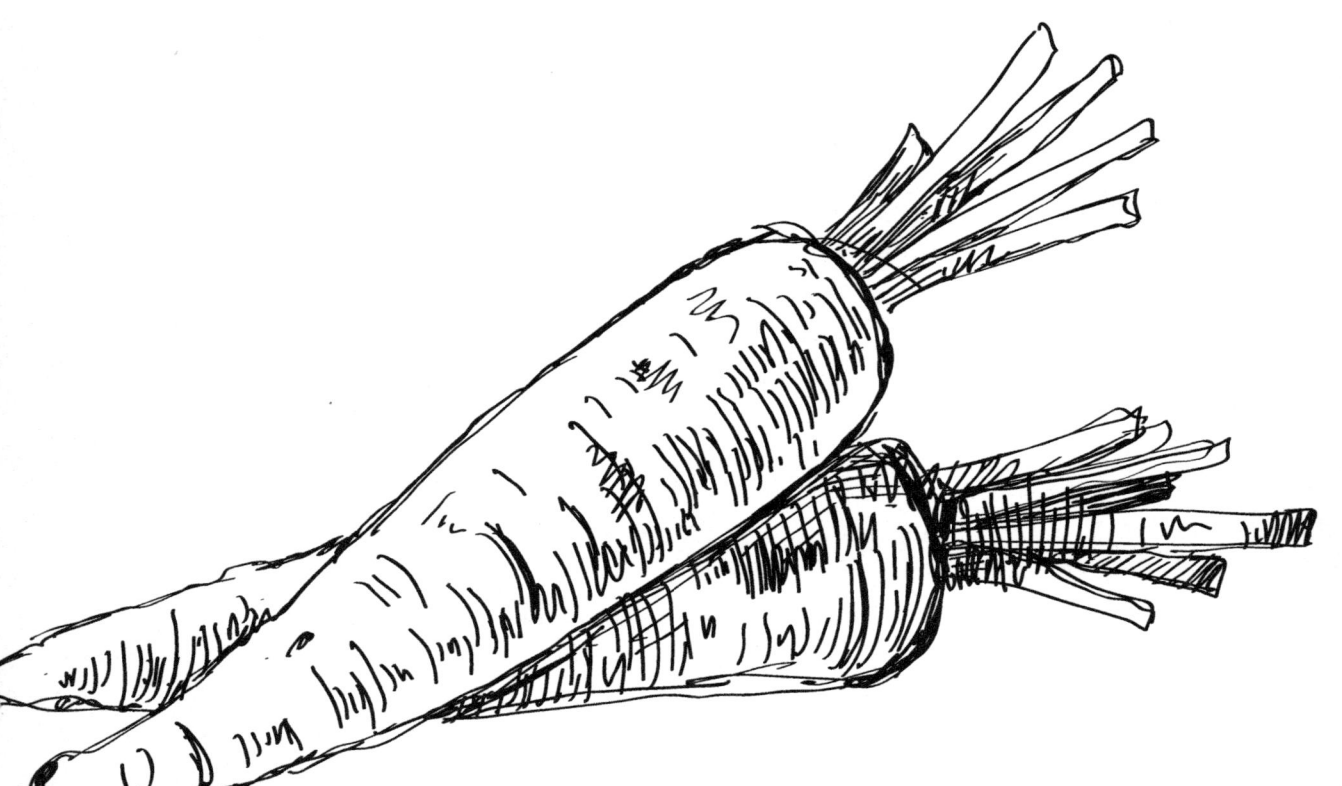

Chicken Kofte Bites

Prep Time: 2 hr
Total Time: 2 hr 30 mins

Servings per Recipe: 2
Calories   412.0
Fat   5.6g
Cholesterol   116.6mg
Sodium   595.1mg
Carbohydrates   48.4g
Protein   41.7g

Ingredients

1 kg ground chicken or 1 kg minced chicken or 1 kg minced beef or 1 kg ground beef
1 1/2 kg potatoes, peeled and finely grated
1 onion, finely chopped
1 egg, whisked (optional)
150 g flat leaf parsley, finely chopped
3 tsp ground cinnamon
3 tsp dried mint, grounded
1 1/8 tsp salt
1 tsp ground black pepper, to taste
Vegetable oil, for frying

Directions

1. Discard the skin of the potatoes and grate them. Toss them in a large mixing bowl with 1/8 tsp of salt. Place it in a colander and let drain for 5 min.
2. Combine the chicken or beef, onion, parsley, egg, cinnamon, mint, salt and black pepper. add the grated and drained potato and combine them well.
3. Shape the mix into medium sized patties and cook them in the hot oil until they become golden brown on both sides. Serve them with a salad.
4. Enjoy.

TURKISH Mozzarella Casserole

 Prep Time: 20 mins
Total Time: 30 mins

Servings per Recipe: 2
Calories   571.6
Fat   34.0g
Cholesterol   165.5mg
Sodium   275.2mg
Carbohydrates   15.1g
Protein   50.8g

Ingredients

3 pieces chicken breasts, cut in cubes
2 tsp extra virgin olive oil
1 tbsp butter
1 medium onion, chopped
1 - 2 garlic clove, minced
5 mixed mushrooms, brushed and thickly sliced
1 red bell pepper, cut in cubes
2 tomatoes, peeled, cut in cubes

salt
pepper
1 tsp oregano
GARNISH
1/4 C. mozzarella cheese
1/2 tsp Turkish red pepper powder

Directions

1. Place skillet over medium heat then melt the butter with olive oil in it. Add the garlic with onion and cook them for 4 min.
2. Stir in the chicken and cook them for an extra 4 min. combine in the mushrooms, tomatoes, cubanelle pepper (red bell pepper), salt and pepper.
3. Lower the heat and put on the lid then cook them for 16 min. once the time is up, remove the skillet from the heat and top it with oregano.
4. Before you do anything else preheat the oven to 400 f.
5. Spoon the chicken mix into a greased casserole dish and top it with the red pepper and mozzarella cheese. cook it in the oven for 5 to 10 min or until the cheese melts. serve it warm.
6. Enjoy.

Allspice Sweet Quinces Stew

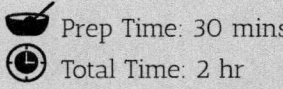
Prep Time: 30 mins
Total Time: 2 hr

Servings per Recipe: 4
Calories	681.5
Fat	42.0g
Cholesterol	135.2mg
Sodium	446.0mg
Carbohydrates	45.6g
Protein	33.3g

Ingredients

- 4 tbsp olive oil
- 2 lbs lamb, fat removed, cut in 1 inch pieces
- 1 large onion, chopped
- 3 tbsp pomegranate molasses
- 1 C. water
- 1/2 tsp ground cinnamon
- 1/2 tsp ground allspice (optional)
- 1/2 tsp salt
- 1/4 tsp ground black pepper
- 2 tbsp butter or 2 tbsp margarine
- 2 lbs quinces, peeled, cored, and quartered
- 2 tbsp brown sugar
- 1 pinch ground cloves (optional) or 1 pinch allspice (optional)
- 1/2 tsp ground cinnamon

Directions

1. Place a large skillet over medium heat and heat 2 tbsp of oil. cook in it the lamb in batches until it become brown.
2. Drain it and place it aside. add 2 tbsp of oil to the skillet and heat it. sauté in it the onion for 6 min.
3. Stir in the pomegranate molasses and the water. add the browned lamb back with the tsp cinnamon, allspice, salt, and pepper. put on the lid and let them cook for 1 h.
4. Place a skillet over medium heat and heat the butter in it. Stir in the quinces and cook them over high heat for 4 min on each side.
5. Stir in the sugar, cloves, and 1/2 tbsp cinnamon. Spoon the quinces mix and place them on over browned lamb mix.
6. Put on the lid and cook them for 32 min over low heat. Serve your lamb quince stew warm.
7. Enjoy.

CHICKEN
Taro Stew

🥣 Prep Time: 10 mins
🕐 Total Time: 55 mins

Servings per Recipe: 4
Calories   609.5
Fat   34.6g
Cholesterol   116.2mg
Sodium   357.8mg
Carbohydrates   40.4g
Protein   34.1g

Ingredients

3 tbsp olive oil
600 g chicken pieces or 600 g chicken breasts, chopped to bite size pieces
400 g taro root, peel dark skin, wash, chopped to bite size pieces
1 large onion, chopped (about 140 grams)
2 tbsp tomato paste
1 (400 g) cans diced tomatoes
2 C. chicken stock, may need more
1 lemon, juice of
Salt, to taste
Black pepper, to taste
GARNISH
Coriander (optional) or cilantro (optional)

Directions

1. Place a large saucepan over medium heat. Heat 1/3 of the olive oil in it and brown in it the chicken for 6 min. drain it and place it aside.
2. Heat another 1/3 of the olive oil in the same saucepan then sauté in it the taro for 5 min. drain it and place it aside.
3. Hear the rest of the olive oil in the saucepan then sauté in it the onion for 3 min. add the chicken back with tomato paste, diced tomatoes & chicken stock.
4. Lower the heat and cook them until they start boiling. Stir in the taro with lemon, a pinch of salt and pepper.
5. Lower the heat and cook the stew for 32 min over low heat then serve it warm.
6. Enjoy.

Turkish Breakfast

Prep Time: 10 mins
Total Time: 20 mins

Servings per Recipe: 1
Calories   278.4
Fat   19.5g
Cholesterol   397.0mg
Sodium   361.8mg
Carbohydrates   9.2g
Protein   16.9g

Ingredients

4 eggs
1 tbsp cream
1 cubanelle pepper, stemmed and chopped
into bite-size pieces
4 -5 medium sized roma tomatoes,
chopped into bite-size pieces
1/2 tbsp extra virgin olive oil
1/4 C. feta cheese, crumbled
Salt and pepper

Directions

1. Place a large skillet over medium heat. Heat the oil in it. Add the peppers and cook them for 3 min over high heat.
2. Drain the tomato and add it to the pan with a pinch of salt and pepper. Let them cook for 9 min.
3. Whisk the cream with eggs, a pinch of salt and pepper in a mixing bowl. Pour the mix all over the tomato mix then cook it until it is done while stirring occasionally. Serve it warm.
4. Enjoy.

LAMB STEW with Turkish Baharat

Prep Time: 5 mins
Total Time: 55 mins

Servings per Recipe: 3
Calories   328.0
Fat   17.9g
Cholesterol   108.5mg
Sodium   170.5mg
Carbohydrates   5.6g
Protein   34.6g

Ingredients
1/2 kg boneless stewing lamb
2 tbsp olive oil
1 medium onion, finely chopped
1 garlic clove, minced
1/4 C. chopped sweet pepper
1/2 C. canned tomatoes, pureed or 3/4 C. chopped peeled tomatoes
3/4 C. water
1/2 tsp baharat, spice mix Baharat Spice Blend or 1/2 tsp ground allspice
Salt
Fresh ground black pepper
1/4 C. chopped parsley

Directions
1. Slice the meat with a sharp knife into dices.
2. Place a large skillet over medium heat. Heat 1 tbsp of olive oil in it then brown in it the lamb in batches.
3. Drain it and place it aside. Heat the rest of oil in the same skillet. Sauté in it the onion with sweet pepper and garlic for 4 min.
4. Stir in the water with tomato, baharat, and a pinch of salt, pepper and some of the parsley.
5. Stir the browned lamb back into the skillet. Put on the lid and cook it for 1 h 35 min. serve your stew warm.
6. Enjoy.

Quick Beef Lunch Skillet

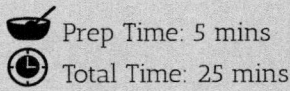 Prep Time: 5 mins
Total Time: 25 mins

Servings per Recipe: 2
Calories   757.9
Fat   55.5g
Cholesterol   177.4mg
Sodium   286.5mg
Carbohydrates   16.2g
Protein   46.5g

Ingredients

2 - 3 C. Baby Spinach, coarsely chopped
1 lb ground beef
2 tbsp olive oil
1 tbsp butter
2 tbsp rice
1 small tomatoes, chopped
1/2-1 tsp red pepper paste
3 tbsp crushed canned tomatoes
salt
pepper
garlic, yogurt sauce
1/2 C. yogurt
1 clove garlic minced. mashed with salt

Directions

1. Place a pot over medium heat. Heat the oil in it with butter. Add the onion and cook it for 4 min.
2. Stir in the beef with a pinch of salt and pepper. Cook them for 8 min.
3. Stir in the rice, tomato, and red pepper paste and crushed tomato. Cover them with the spinach on top then put on the lid and let them cook for 15 min or until the rice is done.
4. Serve your beef skillet warm.
5. Enjoy.

CHEESE AND LAMB
Stuffed Pastry

 Prep Time: 1 hr
Total Time: 1 hr 10 mins

Servings per Recipe: 16
Calories 373.9
Fat 20.1g
Cholesterol 111.8mg
Sodium 548.0mg
Carbohydrates 28.5g
Protein 18.7g

Ingredients

Dough:
100 g butter
200 ml milk, at room temperature
2 tsp sugar
1 tsp salt
20 g fresh yeast
2 eggs
2 egg whites
1000 ml all-purpose flour
Feta Filling (for half the pastries):
1 small onion, chopped
1 garlic clove, chopped
1 tbsp oil
200 g feta cheese
1 egg
100 ml chopped fresh parsley
50 ml chopped fresh dill
50 ml plain yogurt
1/2 tsp salt
black pepper
Beef Filling (for half the pastries):
300 g ground beef
1 onion, chopped
1 garlic clove, chopped
1 tbsp oil
100 ml chopped fresh parsley
1/2 tbsp lemon juice
1 - 2 tsp chili paste
1 1/2 tsp ground paprika
1 tsp sugar
1/2-1 tsp salt
black pepper
1 egg

Directions

1. To prepare the dough:
2. Place a medium saucepan over medium heat and heat the butter in it.
3. Combine in the sugar with salt and sugar in a large saucepan. Heat them until they become warm. Pour the mix into a large mixing bowl.
4. Add the yeast followed by the eggs and egg whites. Mix them well.
5. Combine in the flour gradually then keep your mixing them with your hands until you get a smooth dough.
6. Place the dough in a grease bowl and cover it with a wet towel. Place it aside to rest for 45 f.
7. To prepare the feta cheese filling:

8. Place a skillet over medium heat and heat the oil in it. Add the onion with garlic and cook them for 4 min. place it aside to lose heat.
9. Place the feta cheese in a medium mixing bowl and use a fork to crumble it. Add the cooked onion and garlic with egg, parsley, dill, a pinch of salt and pepper.
10. Mix them well with a fork until they become like a paste.
11. To prepare the beef filling:
12. Place a large skillet over medium heat. Heat the oil in it. Add the onion with garlic and cook them for 4 min.
13. Stir in the paprika with sugar, parsley, chili paste, lemon juice, a pinch of salt and pepper. Place the mix aside to lose heat. Add the egg and stir them well.
14. Before you do anything preheat the oven to 400 f.
15. Grease a working surface with some oil and place the dough on it. Slice into 2 then cut each half into 8 pieces.
16. Roll each portion of dough in the shape of circle then spoon the cheese filling into 8 of them and the beef filling into the other 8 rounds.
17. Roll the dough on top of the filling then pinch the edges to seal the edges with a fork or your hands. Place the galette on a lined up baking sheet. Coat them with a beaten egg.
18. Cook the stuffed galettes in the oven for 12 min. serve them with your favorite toppings.
19. Enjoy.

GREEK STYLE
Feta Salad

Prep Time: 15 mins
Total Time: 15 mins

Servings per Recipe: 4
Calories   198.0
Fat   16.9g
Cholesterol   20.0mg
Sodium   380.9mg
Carbohydrates   8.6g
Protein   4.5g

Ingredients

1 large ripe tomatoes, cored and seeded and diced
1 medium cucumber, peeled and diced
1 medium green bell pepper, seeded and diced
1/2 small red onion, diced
3 tbsp fresh parsley, chopped (optional)
1/2 C. black olives, brine-cured
3 tbsp extra virgin olive oil

1 tbsp red wine vinegar (to taste)
salt and pepper, to taste
3 oz feta cheese, drained and crumbled

Directions

1. Toss the all the ingredients in a mixing bowl then season them with some salt and pepper. Serve your salad and garnish it with olives.
2. Enjoy.

Warm Leeks Salad

Prep Time: 15 mins
Total Time: 1 hr 5 mins

Servings per Recipe: 6
Calories	273.4
Fat	19.5g
Cholesterol	0.0mg
Sodium	389.0mg
Carbohydrates	24.6g
Protein	2.8g

Ingredients

- 1/2 C. olive oil or 1/2 C. vegetable oil
- 2 lbs leeks, white and light green parts only trimmed, cleaned, and thinly sliced (about 10 medium)
- 2 C. peeled seeded and chopped tomatoes (about 1 lb)
- 1 C. vegetable stock or 1 C. water
- 3/4 tsp salt, about
- ground black pepper
- 1 pinch sugar
- 12 -16 pitted black olives
- 2 - 3 tbsp fresh lemon juice

Directions

1. Get a large saucepan over medium heat: heat the oil in it. Sauté in it the leeks for 12 min.
2. Stir in the tomatoes, stock, salt, pepper, and sugar. Put on the lid and cook them for 32 min.
3. Stir in the lemon juice with olives then cook them for 12 min. place it aside to lose heat slightly then serve it.
4. Enjoy.

SAUCY Rice Casserole

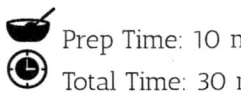
Prep Time: 10 mins
Total Time: 30 mins

Servings per Recipe: 4
Calories 204.7
Fat 3.2g
Cholesterol 7.6mg
Sodium 30.8mg
Carbohydrates 39.5g
Protein 3.5g

Ingredients
1 C. white rice, washed and drained
1 large tomatoes, grated
1 tbsp butter
salt, to taste
Garnish
fresh parsley

Directions
1. Place the rice in a colander and let drain for 2 min.
2. Place a pot over medium heat. Stir in it 2 C. of water with the grated tomato, butter and salt. Cook them until they start boiling.
3. Add the rice then cook them until they start boiling again. Put on the lid and lower the heat then cook them for 18 min over low heat while adding more water if needed.
4. Serve your saucy rice warm.
5. Enjoy.

Turkish Ratatouille

Prep Time: 35 mins
Total Time: 1 hr 5 mins

Servings per Recipe: 2
Calories   474.7
Fat   3.2g
Cholesterol   0.0mg
Sodium   1171.7mg
Carbohydrates   110.4g
Protein   19.7g

Ingredients
2 eggplants
4 onions, peeled and sliced
4 red peppers
4 garlic cloves, sliced
6 tomatoes
2 (5 oz) cans tomato paste
2 green chilies
salt and pepper
oil

Directions
1. Discard several strips of the eggplant skin leaving some on then cut them in half lengthwise. Season them with some salt then place them on a lined up baking sheet.
2. Place a large pot over medium heat. Heat a splash of olive oil in it. Brown in it the eggplant pieces in batches until they become golden brown on both sides.
3. Drain the eggplant pieces and place them in a sieve to remove the excess oil. Repeat the process with the garlic, onion and peppers.
4. Before you do anything else preheat the oven to 450 f.
5. Lay the fried eggplants in glass dish then top it with the fried onion, garlic then red peppers on top.
6. Lay the tomato slices on top then spread then tomato paste on top.
7. Place the veggies casserole in the oven for 40 min. serve it warm with some rice.
8. Enjoy.

VANILLA
Chicken Pudding

Prep Time: 30 mins
Total Time: 50 mins

Servings per Recipe: 6
Calories 430.4
Fat 26.1g
Cholesterol 105.5mg
Sodium 128.6mg
Carbohydrates 39.6g
Protein 10.3g

Ingredients
3/4 C. sugar
1 1/4 C. heavy cream
3 1/2 C. milk
1 tsp vanilla extract
1 boneless skinless chicken breast
5 tbsp rice flour or 5 tbsp cornstarch
1 tbsp butter

Directions
1. Bring a large saucepan of salted water to a boil. Lay the chicken in it and lower the heat. Let the chicken cook for 22 min until it is done.
2. Drain it and place it aside to lose heat. Cut the chicken into bite size pieces.
3. Whisk the flour with a splash of milk in a mixing bowl until they become smooth.
4. Stir the rest of the milk into a large saucepan with the sugar and cream. Cook it until it starts boiling.
5. Add some of the cream mix to the flour mix then whisk it until no lumps are found. Add the mix to the pot while stirring all the time with the vanilla extract.
6. Keep mixing it until it becomes slightly thick then fold into it the shredded chicken.
7. Place a large pan over medium heat. Heat the butter n it then pour the chicken mix into it. Cook it over low heat for 9 min while stirring all the time.
8. Place it aside to lose heat then serve it with some crackers.
9. Enjoy.

Turkish Chicken and Potato Stew

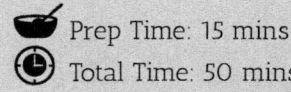

Prep Time: 15 mins
Total Time: 50 mins

Servings per Recipe: 4
Calories	472.5
Fat	20.6g
Cholesterol	46.4mg
Sodium	65.5mg
Carbohydrates	51.7g
Protein	21.2g

Ingredients
- 5 potatoes, cubed
- 2 chicken breasts, cubed
- 2 tomatoes
- 1 medium onion, minced
- 1 tbsp red pepper paste
- 4 tbsp oil

Directions
1. Slice the tomatoes in half and grate them. Discard the skin.
2. Place a large saucepan or pot over medium heat. Stir in it the grated tomato with onions, pepper paste, and oil. Cook them for 5 min.
3. Stir in the potato and cook them for 8 min while stirring often. Stir in the chicken and cook them for 5 min.
4. Pour in 2 C. of hot water to cover the ingredients. Put on the lid and lower the heat then cook them for 26 min over low heat.
5. Serve your stew warm.
6. Enjoy.

ZESTY Carrot Sauté

Prep Time: 15 mins
Total Time: 30 mins

Servings per Recipe: 4
Calories   145.0
Fat   4.0g
Cholesterol   0.0mg
Sodium   518.2mg
Carbohydrates   23.7g
Protein   6.1g

Ingredients

1 tbsp olive oil
3 medium carrots, scrubbed and diced
1 small diced onion
1 1/2 C. tomato sauce
1 freshly-squeezed lemon
2 C. frozen sweet peas
4 cloves garlic, chopped
salt and pepper
1/2 tsp dill weed

Directions

1. Place a large saucepan over saucepan over medium heat. Heat the oil in it. Add the carrots and cook them for 7 min.
2. Stir in the onion and cook them for 3 min.
3. Combine in the tomato sauce with lemon juice, sweet peas, garlic, dill weed, a pinch of salt and pepper. Cook them until they start boiling.
4. Lower the heat and cook them for 10 min until the veggies become tender. Serve it warm.
5. Enjoy.

Hot and Sweet Tomato Spread

Prep Time: 10 mins
Total Time: 1 hr 10 mins

Servings per Recipe: 1
Calories   173.2
Fat   14.0g
Cholesterol   0.0mg
Sodium   19.2mg
Carbohydrates   11.9g
Protein   2.4g

Ingredients

- 1/2 red onions
- 1 tsp sumac
- salt, to taste
- 3 medium tomatoes, seeded, finely chopped
- 1/2 C. fresh parsley, very finely chopped
- 2 tbsp extra virgin olive oil
- 1 tsp pomegranate syrup
- 2 -3 tbsp fresh lemon juice
- 1/2-1 red jalapeno chilis

Directions

1. Get pestle, place it in the sumac with salt and onion. Press them until they become similar to a paste.
2. Transfer the crushed onion mix to a mixing bowl with the olive oil, tomato, syrup, chilis, lemon juice, a pinch of salt and pepper.
3. Place the mix aside to sit for 2 hr then serve it with some nachos, crackers...
4. Enjoy.

REFRESHING
Watermelon Salad

 Prep Time: 10 mins
Total Time: 10 mins

Servings per Recipe: 6
Calories 188.6
Fat 15.3g
Cholesterol 22.4mg
Sodium 147.2mg
Carbohydrates 7.1g
Protein 6.6g

Ingredients

1 lb seedless watermelon, chunks cut into small slabs
6 oz. fresh goat cheese, cut into 12 rounds
1/4 tsp finely grated orange zest
1 tsp nigella seeds (optional)
2 tbsp fresh orange juice
1 tbsp fresh lemon juice
3 tbsp extra virgin olive oil
salt & freshly ground black pepper

Directions

1. Get a small mixing bowl: mix in it the lemon juice with olive oil, orange juice, a pinch of salt and pepper to make the vinaigrette.
2. Place the watermelon chunks on serving plates then top them with the cheese slices, orange zest and nigella seeds.
3. Drizzle the vinaigrette on top then serve your salad.
4. Enjoy.

Cheesy Eggplant Stuffed Pasties

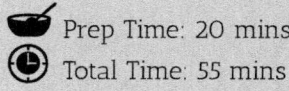 Prep Time: 20 mins
Total Time: 55 mins

Servings per Recipe: 10
Calories 234.9
Fat 14.2g
Cholesterol 29.5mg
Sodium 252.6mg
Carbohydrates 22.2g
Protein 4.9g

Ingredients

Dough:
- 1/2 C. vegetable oil
- 1/4 C. warm water
- 1/2 tsp salt
- 2 C. flour
- 1 egg yolk, mixed with 1 tsp water, for glazing
- 3 tbsp grated kashkaval (optional) or 3 tbsp parmesan cheese (optional)

Eggplant Filling:
- 1 lb eggplant
- 4 oz feta cheese
- 1 C. grated kashkaval, gruyere or 1 C. parmesan cheese
- salt and pepper, as desired

Directions

1. Whisk the salt with oil and water in a mixing bowl. Add some flour and mix them until you get an oily dough.
2. Pierce the eggplants several times with a fork then broil them in the oven until they become tender.
3. Once the time is up, place the eggplants aside to lose heat. Discard their skin and place them in a colander then press them to smash them.
4. Drain them and transfer them to a large mixing bowl. Add the feta and gruyere cheese, a pinch of salt and pepper then combine them well.
5. Split the dough into 2 portions and spread each one of them into large thin circles then cut them in the shape of 4 inches circles.
6. place 1 tbsp of the filling in the middle of each dough circle then roll the dough around it to make in the shape of a half circle. Press the edges to seal them.
7. Before you do anything preheat the oven to 350 F.
8. Place the pasties on lined up baking sheet and brush them with the beaten egg mix. Sprinkle some extra cheese on top then cook them for 37 min.
9. Allow the pasties to cool down slightly then serve them.
10. Enjoy.

TAGINE STYLE
Lamb Stew

Prep Time: 30 mins
Total Time: 1 hr 30 mins

Servings per Recipe: 6
Calories   355.4
Fat   19.5g
Cholesterol   90.1mg
Sodium   880.1mg
Carbohydrates   22.1g
Protein   25.6g

Ingredients
2 small eggplants, sliced
2 tsp salt
2 tbsp butter
2 lbs lamb, cut in 1-inch cubes
2 onions, sliced
1/2 lb green beans, cut in half
3 small zucchini or 2 medium zucchini, sliced thick
4 medium tomatoes, peeled and quartered
fresh ground pepper
2 tbsp chopped parsley

Directions
1. Season the eggplant slices with 1 tsp of salt. Place them in a colander to sit for 20 min. pour on them some water to remove the salt and pat them dry.
2. Place a large ovenproof pan over medium heat. Melt the butter in it. Brown in it the lamb pieces for 8 min. drain it and place it aside.
3. Stir in the onion into the same pan and cook them for 3 min. add the breads with zucchini and tomato, 1 tsp of salt and a pinch of pepper.
4. Place the lamb pieces on top followed by the eggplant slices. Season them with paprika then pour on them enough water to cover them.
5. Before you do anything else preheat the oven to 350 F.
6. Cook the lamb pan until it starts boiling then cook it in the oven for 1 h. serve it warm.
7. Enjoy.

Turkish Style Nuts Pilaf

Prep Time: 15 mins
Total Time: 1 hr 15 mins

Servings per Recipe: 1
Calories   234.6
Fat   11.8g
Cholesterol   0.0mg
Sodium   4.4mg
Carbohydrates   23.6g
Protein   4.8g

Ingredients

- 2 tbsp olive oil
- 1 onion, finely chopped about 1/2 tsp. salt
- 1/3 C. slivered almonds
- 1/3 C. pistachios, halves
- 1/3 C. chopped walnuts
- 3 garlic cloves, minced
- 1 tsp ground coriander
- 1/2 tsp ground cumin
- 1/2 tsp fresh ground black pepper
- 1 C. long grain brown rice (or basmati brown rice)
- 1 C. dry white wine
- 2 1/2 C. reduced-chicken or 2 1/2 C. vegetable broth
- 2 tbsp minced flat leaf parsley (optional)

Directions

1. Place a large skillet over medium heat. Heat the olive oil in it. Sauté in it the onion with 1/2 tsp salt for 4 min.
2. Turn the heat to high. Stir in the almonds, pistachios, and walnuts. Let them cook for 2 min. add the garlic and cook them for 40 sec.
3. Stir in the cumin with coriander and a pinch of pepper. Cook them for another 40 sec. stir in the rice with wine and cook them for 3 min while stirring all the time.
4. Combine in the broth with a pinch of salt. Stir them well then serve your rice pilaf warm.
5. Enjoy.

TURKISH
Dill Patties

🥣 Prep Time: 35 mins
🕐 Total Time: 40 mins

Servings per Recipe: 16
Calories   52.8
Fat   2.1g
Cholesterol   28.8mg
Sodium   82.2mg
Carbohydrates   5.9g
Protein   2.6g

Ingredients

600 g zucchini, grated
sea salt
1 small onion, grated
1 small garlic clove, finely chopped
100 g feta cheese, crumbled
1/4 C. dill, finely chopped
2 tbsp parsley, finely chopped flat-leaf
2 eggs, well beaten
1/2 C. plain flour

2 tbsp rice flour
black pepper, freshly ground
olive oil
lemon wedge (optional)

Directions

1. Place the zucchini in a sieve then season it with a pinch of salt. Place it aside to drain for 30 min.
2. Pour on it some water to rinse it then press it with your hands to remove the water from it. Place it in another colander for 5 min to dry.
3. Toss it with the onion, garlic, feta, herbs and eggs. Mix them well. Add the flour with a pinch of salt and pepper then stir them well.
4. Place a large pan over medium heat. Heat a splash of olive oil in it. Use a tbsp to scoop the mix and the drop it in the hot oil in the shape of patties.
5. Cook them for 2 to 3 min on each side or until they become golden brown. Serve your zucchini patties warm.
6. Enjoy.

Chili Pea Soup

Prep Time:	10 mins
Total Time:	1 hr 10 mins

Servings per Recipe:	3
Calories	491.4
Fat	23.8g
Cholesterol	20.5mg
Sodium	432.8mg
Carbohydrates	51.1g
Protein	20.9g

Ingredients

- 2 tbsp vegetable oil
- 4 -6 slices turkey bacon, cooked and crumbled
- 1 tsp chili flakes
- 1 large white onion, finely chopped
- 2 stalks celery, finely chopped
- 1 C. finely chopped carrot
- 4 tbsp tomato sauce
- 3 stalks fresh thyme
- 1 bay leaf
- 1 C. yellow split peas
- 6 -7 C. water
- salt
- pepper

Directions

1. Place a large saucepan over medium heat. Heat the oil in it. Brown in it the bacon pieces with chili flakes for 10 sec.
2. Stir in the carrot with onion and celery. Cook them for 5 min. add the tomato sauce and cook them for 2 min while stirring all the time.
3. Combine in the thyme, bay leaf and peas, a pinch of salt and pepper.
4. Stir in 2 1/2 C. of water into the saucepan then put on the lid and cook the soup for 22 min over low heat.
5. Once the time is up, stir in another C. of water and let the soup cook for an extra 22 min while adding more water if needed until the peas are done.
6. Turn off the heat and place the soup aside to cool down. Discard the bay leaf.
7. Get a food processor: pour the soup into it and pulse it several times until it becomes chunky. Serve your soup warm.
8. Enjoy.

TURKISH
Pumpkin Candy

Prep Time: 72 hr
Total Time: 74 hr

Servings per Recipe: 32
Calories 58.1
Fat 0.0g
Cholesterol 0.0mg
Sodium 19.6mg
Carbohydrates 14.9g
Protein 0.3g

Ingredients
2 1/4 lbs fresh pumpkin, peeled and cut into 2-inch chunks
1 1/2 C. sugar
1/2 C. light brown sugar
1/4 tsp sea salt
2 tsp cinnamon
1/2 tsp allspice
1/2 tsp cardamom
1/2 tsp ground ginger
1/4 tsp ground cloves

Directions
1. Get a large storage container. Place in it the pumpkin dices and top them with the sugar, spices and salt.
2. Put on the lid and place the container in the fridge for 3 days or 4 while stirring gently every day.
3. Once the time is up, spoon the mix into a large heavy saucepan. Cook them until they start boiling.
4. Lower the heat and cook them for 1 h 45 min over low heat while stirring every once in a while.
5. Once the time is up, then syrupy candy lose heat completely then transfer it storing jars. Serve it or store it in the fridge for more than 2 months.
6. Enjoy.

Saucy Eggplant Casserole

Prep Time: 20 mins
Total Time: 2 hr 20 mins

Servings per Recipe: 6
Calories   252.1
Fat   20.5g
Cholesterol   21.8mg
Sodium   54.8mg
Carbohydrates   14.8g
Protein   4.4g

Ingredients
2 eggplants
600 g beef, diced
6 large garlic cloves, chopped
1 large onion
2 tomatoes, sliced
2 tbsp olive oil
2 tbsp tomato paste, for spaghetti sauce

Directions
1. Cut the eggplants into slices. Place it in a salted bowl of water and let it sit for 22 min. run it under some water and drain it.
2. Place an over large skillet over medium heat and heat the oil in it. Lay in it the meat followed by the garlic, onion, tomato, eggplant, olive oil, tomato paste and a pinch of salt.
3. Before you do anything preheat the oven to 400 F.
4. Place the skillet in the oven for 16 min. once the time is up, pour into it 4 C. of water.
5. Place it back in the oven and let it cook for 1 h 32 min or until the meat and veggies are done. Serve it warm.
6. Enjoy.

EASY PEASY
Chickpea Falafels

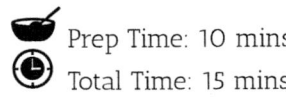

Prep Time: 10 mins
Total Time: 15 mins

Servings per Recipe: 4
Calories 157.0
Fat 1.3g
Cholesterol 0.0mg
Sodium 611.8mg
Carbohydrates 30.5g
Protein 6.2g

Ingredients

- 1 (15 oz) cans chickpeas, drained
- 1 medium onion, finely chopped
- 1 tbsp minced garlic
- 2 tbsp fresh parsley, finely chopped
- 1 tsp coriander
- 3/4 tsp cumin
- 1/2 tsp salt
- 2 tbsp flour
- canola oil (for frying) or vegetable oil (for frying)

Directions

1. Get a mixing bowl: toss in it the chickpeas, garlic, onion, coriander, flour, cumin, salt and pepper.
2. Use a fork or a potato masher to mash them until they are well combined. Shape the mix into medium sized patties and place them on a lined up baking sheet.
3. Place a large skillet over medium heat and fill 2 inches of it with oil then heat it until it start sizzling.
4. Drop in it the chickpea falafels and cook them on both sides until they become golden brown. Serve them with your favorite toppings.
5. Enjoy.

Chicken Flavored Leeks Stew

Prep Time: 10 mins
Total Time: 50 mins

Servings per Recipe: 4
Calories 288.9
Fat 11.4g
Cholesterol 0.0mg
Sodium 534.3mg
Carbohydrates 44.3g
Protein 6.2g

Ingredients

2 lbs leeks, outer leaves and root ends removed
3 tbsp olive oil
3 medium onions, sliced thin
3 tomatoes, peeled & chopped
1/2 tsp salt
fresh ground pepper
1 C. chicken broth or 1 C. chicken bouillon
2 tbsp chopped fresh dill or 1 tbsp dried dill

Directions

1. Slice the leeks in half crosswise.
2. Get a pot: heat the oil in it then sauté in it the onion for 4 min. combine in the leeks and cook them for another 4 min.
3. Combine in the broth with tomato then cook them until they start boiling. Lower the heat and cook them for 32 min.
4. Turn off the heat then serve your stew warm.
5. Enjoy.

SESAME Bread Wheels

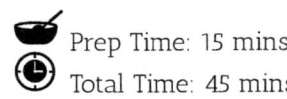

Prep Time: 15 mins
Total Time: 45 mins

Servings per Recipe: 4
Calories   399.4
Fat   20.2g
Cholesterol   47.0mg
Sodium   736.6mg
Carbohydrates   45.3g
Protein   8.9g

Ingredients

8 oz. plain white flour (225g)
1 tsp salt
2 oz. margarine (50g) or 2 oz. butter (50g)
1 tbsp oil
1 tbsp milk
1 tbsp water
1 egg, beaten
1 oz. sesame seeds (25g) or 1 oz. poppy seed, approximately (25g)

Directions

1. Before you do anything preheat the oven to 400 F.
2. Get a large mixing bowl: combine in it the flour with salt. Add the oil with butter, milk, egg and water in the middle.
3. Mix them with a whisk until they are well combined then use your hands to knead the dough until it becomes soft.
4. Transfer the dough to a floured surface and roll it with a rolling pin then cut into 4 inches rings.
5. Lay the dough wheels on greased baking sheets then brush them with some milk. Sprinkle the sesame seeds on them.
6. Cook the sesame wheels in the oven for 32 min. serve them warm.
7. Enjoy.

Creamy Nectarine Chocolate Parfait

Prep Time: 15 mins
Total Time: 15 mins

Servings per Recipe: 6
Calories   382.3
Fat   24.5g
Cholesterol   90.6mg
Sodium   73.3mg
Carbohydrates   33.6g
Protein   8.8g

Ingredients

- 400 g ricotta cheese
- 165 g caster sugar
- 300 ml thickened cream
- 100 g white chocolate Toblerone chocolate bars, chopped finely
- 100 g Turkish Delight, chopped finely
- 150 g chopped nectarines

Directions

1. Combine the sugar with ricotta cheese in large mixing bowl. Mix them with an electric mixer until they become light and fluffy.
2. Pour the cream into a mixing bowl. Mix it with an electric mixer until it soft peaks.
3. Fold the chocolate with Turkish delight and nectarines into the mix followed the cream.
4. Line up a casserole dish with a piece of foil then pour the cream mix into it and spread it. Place another piece of foil on top to cover it.
5. Place it in the freeze for 8 to 12 h. once the time is up, remove the frozen cream delight from the casserole dish and let sit for 16 min.
6. Cut with a sharp knife into slices and serve it.
7. Enjoy.

BELL MARINATED
Lamb Kebab

🥣 Prep Time: 30 mins
🕐 Total Time: 40 mins

Servings per Recipe: 6
Calories 655.4
Fat 31.2g
Cholesterol 129.4mg
Sodium 1163.2mg
Carbohydrates 54.8g
Protein 37.1g

Ingredients

1 lb ground lamb
1 lb ground veal
4 tsp olive oil, for brushing on pita's
4 tsp salted butter, small cubes
1 red bell pepper, minced
1 medium yellow onion, minced
3 garlic cloves, minced
1 C. yogurt
2 medium red onions, sliced very thin

1 tsp sumac
1 tsp lemon juice
8 pieces pita bread or 8 pieces naan bread
2 tsp red pepper flakes
2 tsp ground coriander
2 tsp cumin
2 tsp black pepper
2 tsp kosher salt
2 tsp sumac

Directions

1. Stir the bell peppers with onion, veal and lamb, spices, a pinch of salt and pepper. Cover the bowl with a piece of plastic wrap. Place it in the fridge for 8 h.
2. Before you do anything preheat the grill and grease its grates.
3. Whisk the red onion, sumac, and yogurt and lemon juice. Put on the lid and place it in the fridge to make the sauce.
4. Shape the meat mix into medium sized logs and thread them into skewers. Grill them for 4 to 5 min on each side or until they are done.
5. Serve your lamb kebabs with pita bread and yogurt sauce.
6. Enjoy.

Walnut Egg Noodles Salad

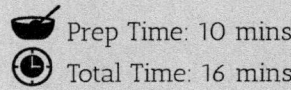
Prep Time: 10 mins
Total Time: 16 mins

Servings per Recipe: 4
Calories 397.4
Fat 18.9 g
Cholesterol 124.2 mg
Sodium 381.9 mg
Carbohydrates 45.5 g
Protein 12.1 g

Ingredients
2 C. wide egg noodles
1 bunch arugula, washed, drained, ripped
2 tbsp butter
salt
fresh crack black pepper
Garnish:
1/2 C. toasted walnuts, coarsely chopped
thick yogurt
fresh parsley, minced
Egg Noodles:
1 1/4 C. flour
1/2 tsp salt
2 eggs, lightly beaten

Directions
1. Cook the noodles according to the directions on the package.
2. Place a large saucepan over medium heat. Heat the butter in it. Sauté in it the egg noodles with a pinch of salt and pepper for 3 to 5 min.
3. Stir in the arugula and cook them for 1 min while stirring all the time. Turn off the heat.
4. Spoon the noodles into a serving plate then top it with yogurt and walnuts.
5. To prepare homemade egg noodles:
6. Combine the salt with flour in a large mixing bowl. Make a well in the middle of it. Place in it the eggs and mix them with a fork gradually until they are combined.
7. Transfer the dough to a floured working surface and knead the dough with your hands until it becomes soft. Shape it into a bowl and cover it with a wet cloth.
8. Allow the dough to rest for 32 min. cut it into 3 portions. Place them on a floured surface and roll them until in the shape of a rectangular until they become thin.
9. Cut the dough rectangular into 1 cm wide strips with a sharp knife or pizza cutter.
10. Bring a large pot of water to a boil. Add the noodles to it and put on the lid. Cook it until it start boiling again.
11. Let the noodles cook for another 4 to 6 min. drain it and prepare it the way you desire.
12. Enjoy.

FETA FRITTERS
with Creamy Cucumber Sauce

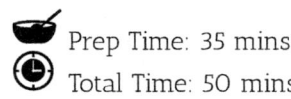

Prep Time: 35 mins
Total Time: 50 mins

Servings per Recipe: 3
Calories   199.9
Fat   12.6g
Cholesterol   161.4mg
Sodium   818.7mg
Carbohydrates   9.8g
Protein   12.8g

Ingredients

Yogurt Sauce:
1 C. plain yogurt
1/4 C. cucumber, finely diced
2 tbsp fresh dill, chopped
1 tbsp lime juice
1 garlic clove, grated (optional)
salt
pepper
Fritters:

2 1/2 C. zucchini
4 tbsp green onions, chopped
2 tbsp fresh dill, chopped
2 eggs
4 tbsp gluten-free flour or 4 tbsp rice flour
1/2 tsp salt
3 oz feta cheese, crumbled
oil

Directions

1. Grate the zucchini and press it with your hands to remove the excess water from it.
2. Get a small mixing bowl: stir in it the yogurt, cucumber, dill, lime juice, garlic, salt and pepper to make the sauce. Place it in the fridge.
3. Get a large mixing bowl: combine in it the shredded zucchini with green onions, dill, eggs, flour and salt. Stir in the cheese.
4. Place a large skillet over medium heat. Heat a splash of oil in it. Spoon 1/6 of the zucchini mix with a large tbsp and drop it in the hot oil in a round shape.
5. Repeat the process with the rest of the mix to make several patties. Cook them for 3 to 5 min on each side until they become golden brown on each side.
6. Serve your zucchini patties with the cucumber sauce.
7. Enjoy.

Warm Veggies and Butter Beans Stew

Prep Time: 5 mins
Total Time: 30 mins

Servings per Recipe: 4
Calories   356.7
Fat   14.9g
Cholesterol   1.8mg
Sodium   645.7mg
Carbohydrates   45.5g
Protein   11.8g

Ingredients

1/4 C. olive oil
1 onion, chopped
2 cloves garlic, minced
1 large tomatoes, chopped (optional)
1 medium carrot, peeled and diced
1 medium potato, peeled and diced
1 stalk celery, thinly sliced
1 C. chicken stock
2 (15 oz) cans butter beans, drained
2 tbsp lemon juice
1 tbsp fresh parsley
salt and pepper, to taste

Directions

1. Place a large heavy saucepan over medium heat. Heat the oil in it. Sauté in it the garlic with onion for 4 min.
2. Stir in the carrot with celery, tomato and potato. Cook them for 5 min. stir in the stock and cook them for 12 min.
3. Once the time is up, combine in the beans, lemon juice, a pinch of salt and pepper. Cook the stew for an extra 12 min over low heat.
4. Fold in the parsley. Serve your stew warm with some rice.
5. Enjoy.

TURKISH
Vanilla Cake

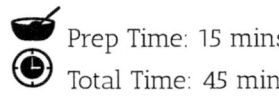

Prep Time: 15 mins
Total Time: 45 mins

Servings per Recipe: 24
Calories 157.4
Fat 7.4g
Cholesterol 23.2mg
Sodium 59.6mg
Carbohydrates 20.9g
Protein 2.0g

Ingredients
150 -200 g spinach
3/4 C. extra virgin olive oil
2 tbsp lemon juice
1 tsp vanilla essence
3 eggs
1 1/2 C. sugar
2 C. flour
3 tsp baking powder

Directions
1. Before you do anything preheat the oven to 350 F.
2. Get a blender: combine in it the spinach, olive oil, vanilla and lemon juice. Process them until they become smooth.
3. Combine in the sugar with eggs and process them again.
4. Mix the flour with baking powder in a large mixing bowl. Pour in the vanilla and spinach mix. Stir them until no lumps are found.
5. Grease a 9 inches cake pan with some butter and flour it. Pour the cake batter into it and bake it for 32 min.
6. Allow the cake to cool down completely then serve it with your favorite toppings.
7. Enjoy.

Ajvar Chicken Stew

Prep Time: 15 mins
Total Time: 2 hrs

Servings per Recipe: 6
Calories   196.4
Fat   7.6g
Cholesterol   72.6mg
Sodium   232.1mg
Carbohydrates   5.8g
Protein   25.8g

Ingredients

- 2 tbsp olive oil, divided
- 1 1/2 lbs boneless skinless chicken breasts, cut into 1 inch cubes or 1 1/2 lbs chicken legs with thigh
- 0.5 (12 oz) Ajvar
- 1 (14 1/2 oz) cans diced tomatoes with juice
- 1 (6 oz) jars mushrooms, drained
- 1 onion, diced
- 1 tbsp garlic, minced
- salt and pepper, to taste

Directions

1. Place a large pot over medium heat. Heat 1 tbsp of oil in it. Brown in it the chicken for 8 min.
2. Stir in the chicken, ajvar, tomatoes, mushrooms, onion, and garlic, a pinch of salt and pepper. Add the rest of the oil to them.
3. Cook them until they start boiling. Put on the lid and cook them for 1 h 35 min over low heat.
4. Once the time is up, serve your chicken stew warm.
5. Enjoy.

SPICY CHICKEN Kabobs with Pomegranate Relish

Prep Time: 35 mins
Total Time: 1 hr 35 mins

Servings per Recipe: 4
Calories 530.9
Fat 35.5g
Cholesterol 75.5mg
Sodium 154.1mg
Carbohydrates 23.8g
Protein 33.3g

Ingredients

Tahini Yogurt:
3 1/2 tbsp fresh lemon juice
1 tbsp baharat seasoning
1 large garlic clove, pressed
1/2 C. plain whole-milk Greek yogurt
1/4 C. tahini
Relish":
1 1/4 C. pomegranate seeds
2/3 C. pistachios, coarsely chopped, shelled unsalted natural
1/3 C. fresh Italian parsley, coarsely chopped
2 1/2 tbsp olive oil
2 1/2 tsp fresh lemon juice
Chicken:
1/2 C. coarsely grated onion
2 tbsp fresh lemon juice
2 tbsp olive oil
2 tsp baharat seasoning
4 boneless skinless chicken breast halves, each halved lengthwise, then cut crosswise into 3 pieces
For Serving:
warm pita bread

Directions

1. To make the yogurt sauce:
2. Get a mixing bowl: pour in it the lemon juice, Baharat seasoning, and garlic. Mix them with a fork and stir in the tahini with a pinch of salt. Place it aside.
3. To make the relish:
4. Get a mixing bowl: stir in it the pomegranate seeds with parsley, lemon juice, olive oil and pistachios with a pinch of salt. Place it aside to sit for 2 h.
5. To make the chicken kabobs:
6. Get a large mixing bowl: mix in it the onion with oil, Baharat seasoning and lemon juice.
7. Add the chicken and place it aside to sit for 2 h.
8. Before you do anything else preheat the oven broiler.
9. Thread the chicken pieces into skewers and then season them with some salt and pepper.
10. Place them on a greased baking sheet and cook them in the oven for 7 min on each side. Serve them warm with the pomegranate relish and yogurt sauce.
11. Enjoy.

Double Stuffed Eggplants

🥣 Prep Time: 30 mins
🕐 Total Time: 1 hr 20 mins

Servings per Recipe: 6
Calories   253.8
Fat   10.8g
Cholesterol   0.0mg
Sodium   564.4mg
Carbohydrates   36.0g
Protein   6.4g

Ingredients

- 2 medium eggplants (about 1-1/4 lbs. each)
- 4 tbsp olive oil
- 2 medium onions, chopped (about 2 C.)
- 4 garlic cloves, minced
- 4 large tomatoes, seeded and chopped (about 6 C.)
- 1 1/4 C. Italian-style dry breadcrumbs, divided
- 1 tsp salt
- 1 1/2 tsp pepper
- 3/4 C. water

Directions

1. Before you do anything preheat the oven to 350 F.
2. Slice the eggplants in half. Spoon out the flesh of the eggplant while reserving the shell intact.
3. Place the eggplant shells in a greased casserole dish and drizzle some olive oil on them. Place them aside.
4. Slice the eggplant flesh into dices. Place a large saucepan over medium heat. Heat the oil in it. Cook in it the onion for 6 min.
5. Stir in the garlic and cook them for 2 min. add the tomato and let them cook for an extra 9 min.
6. Stir in 1 C. of breadcrumbs with a pinch of salt and pepper to make the filling. Spoon the mix into the eggplant shells and sprinkle on them the remaining breadcrumbs.
7. Add the water to the casserole dish then cook it in the oven for 55 min. once the time is up, serve it warm.
8. Enjoy.

SAFFRON
Rice Kebab

Prep Time: 1 hr 30 mins
Total Time: 2 hr

Servings per Recipe: 4
Calories 784.0
Fat 27.6g
Cholesterol 144.0mg
Sodium 111.0mg
Carbohydrates 84.0g
Protein 45.2g

Ingredients
600 g fatter mutton, diced
1 lemon, juice of
2 onions
200 g rice
salt and pepper
1 tsp saffron

Directions
1. Stir the meat with onion and lemon juice in a large mixing bowl. Place it aside to sit for 60 min.
2. Place a large saucepan over medium heat and heat the oil in it. Add the rice and coo kit for 2 min. stir in the water with saffron in a mixing bowl then add them to the rice.
3. Lower the heat and cook them until the rice is done.
4. Preheat the grill and grease its grates. Thread the lamb dices into skewers then drizzle on them some oil. Cook them for 5 to 7 min on each side. Serve them warm.
5. Enjoy.

Hot Molasses Dip

Prep Time: 2 mins
Total Time: 5 mins

Servings per Recipe: 1
Calories	1107.5
Fat	38.6g
Cholesterol	0.0mg
Sodium	142.3mg
Carbohydrates	188.8g
Protein	14.2g

Ingredients
- 1/2 C. grape molasses
- 1/4 C. tahini

Directions
1. Stir in the all the ingredients in a small mixing bowl.
2. Serve it with some bread.
3. Enjoy.

TOFU
Dessert Salad

🥣 Prep Time: 45 mins
🕐 Total Time: 45 mins

Servings per Recipe: 4
Calories   340.9
Fat   8.9g
Cholesterol   0.0mg
Sodium   1234.5mg
Carbohydrates   54.3g
Protein   15.8g

Ingredients

12 oz. firm tofu
15 oz. canned chick-peas
1/2 C. apricot
1/2 C. grapes
1/4 C. prune
1 medium onion
1/4 C. slivered almonds
3 figs
1/2 tsp saffron thread

1 1/2 tbsp flour
1 1/2 tsp salt
1/4 C. sugar-free syrup
1 tsp poppy seed

Directions

1. Place a large heavy saucepan over medium heat. Stir in it the fruits with tofu and onion and syrup. Cook them for 10 min.
2. Drain the cooked tofu, fruit and veggies mix and place it aside. Add the flour to remaining syrup in the pan and stir it well. Cook until it thickens.
3. Stir the tofu mix back into the saucepan with a pinch of salt and pepper then cook them for another 10 min over low heat. Serve it with warm with poppy seeds on top.
4. Enjoy.

Sultan's Delight Stew

Prep Time: 30 mins
Total Time: 2 hrs

Servings per Recipe: 6
Calories   366.7
Fat   24.5g
Cholesterol   91.7mg
Sodium   145.7mg
Carbohydrates   17.0g
Protein   20.7g

Ingredients

Stew
- 1 large onion, sliced
- 1 tbsp vegetable oil
- 1 1/2 lbs lamb, cut into 3/4 inch cubes
- 2 garlic cloves, chopped
- 1 lb tomatoes, peeled and chopped
- 1 tsp sugar

Eggplant Sauce
- 1 lb eggplant
- 2 tbsp lemon juice
- 4 tbsp butter
- 2 tbsp all-purpose flour
- 2 C. hot milk
- 1/4 tsp grated nutmeg
- 1/2 C. kasseri cheese, grated

Directions

1. Place a large pot over medium heat. Heat the oil in it. Add the onion and cook it for 3 min. stir in the meat and cook them for 6 min. stir in the garlic and cook them for 40 sec.
2. Stir in the sugar with tomato, a pinch of salt and pepper. Pour in the water then put on the lid and let them cook for 1 h 25 min while adding water if needed.
3. To make the eggplant:
4. Before you do anything preheat the oven to 500 F.
5. Pierce the eggplants with a fork several times. Place them on a lined up baking sheet and cook them for 32 min.
6. Place the eggplants aside to lose heat for a while then peel them.
7. Fill a bowl with water and stir into it some lemon juice then place in it the eggplants.
8. Place a large saucepan over medium heat. Heat the butter in it. Add the flour and stir it while cooking for 2 min.
9. Turn off the heat and combine the milk gradually while whisking all the time. Stir in the nutmeg powder with a pinch of salt and pepper.
10. Let them cook for 16 min over low heat while stirring from time to time until you get a thick sauce.
11. Remove the eggplants from the water and pat them dry then transfer them to a mixing bowl. Mash them with a potato masher.
12. Transfer the eggplant to the saucepan with the milk mix then mix them well. Heat them over medium heat then stir in the cheese until it melts.
13. Adjust the seasoning of the sauce then serve it over the lamb stew warm.
14. Enjoy.

TURKISH Fish Stew

Prep Time: 15 mins
Total Time: 45 mins

Servings per Recipe: 4
Calories	456 kcal
Carbohydrates	53.4 g
Cholesterol	42 mg
Fat	12.4 g
Fiber	6.3 g
Protein	32.7 g
Sodium	755 mg

Ingredients
- 3 cups water
- 1 1/2 cups dry couscous
- 2 tbsps olive oil
- 1 small white onion, chopped
- 1 green bell pepper, chopped
- 2 cloves garlic, minced
- 1 cup marinated artichoke hearts, liquid reserved
- 2 tsps capers, liquid reserved
- 12 small green olives
- 1 (14.5 ounce) can chopped stewed tomatoes, drained
- 2 tbsps fish stock
- 1 tbsp lemon juice
- 1 cup water
- 2 tsps sumac powder
- 1 1/2 tsps crushed red pepper flakes
- 1 tsp dried basil
- 1 tsp cumin
- 1 tsp minced fresh ginger root
- ground black pepper to taste
- 1 pound tilapia fillets, cut into chunks

Directions
1. Add couscous into boiling water before turning the heat off and letting it stand as it is for about 5 minutes.
2. Cook onion and green pepper in hot olive oil for about five minutes before adding garlic and cooking it for another two minutes.
3. Stir in artichoke hearts, capers and some olives before adding tomatoes, water, fish stock, red pepper, ginger, pepper, cumin, sumac powder, basil and lemon juice before bringing this all to boil.
4. Stir in fish chunks before turning the heat down and cooking all this for another ten minutes.
5. Serve this over couscous in a platter.

Haydari
(A Turkish Yogurt Dip)

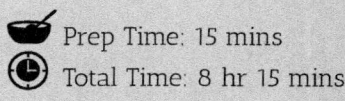

Prep Time: 15 mins
Total Time: 8 hr 15 mins

Servings per Recipe: 6	
Calories	92 kcal
Carbohydrates	5.7 g
Cholesterol	19 mg
Fat	5.9 g
Fiber	0.4 g
Protein	4.5 g
Sodium	88 mg

Ingredients
1 (16 ounce) container plain yogurt
5 cloves garlic
1 pinch salt
1 bunch fresh dill, chopped
1 bunch fresh parsley, chopped
1 (4 ounce) package cream cheese, softened (optional)
2 mint leaves, for garnish

Directions
1. Place a colander having cheesecloth over a medium sized bowl and put yoghurt on the cheesecloth before covering the colander with plastic wrap and letting it stand as it is for 8 hours.
2. Add mashed salt and garlic in a bowl containing drained yoghurt before adding cream cheese, dill and parsley into it.
3. Place it on serving dish and garnish with mint leaves before serving.

TAVA I
(A Turkish Stew)

Prep Time: 15 mins
Total Time: 55 mins

Servings per Recipe: 6	
Calories	397 kcal
Carbohydrates	9.4 g
Cholesterol	113 mg
Fat	19.5 g
Fiber	1.8 g
Protein	43.7 g
Sodium	854 mg

Ingredients

2 tbsps olive oil, divided
1 1/2 pounds skinless, boneless chicken breast halves - cut into 1 inch cubes
1/2 (12 ounce) jar roasted red bell peppers, drained
1 (14.5 ounce) can diced tomatoes with juice
1 (6 ounce) jar mushrooms, drained
1 onion, diced
1 tbsp minced garlic
salt and pepper to taste
1 (16 ounce) package shredded mozzarella cheese

Directions

1. Preheat your oven to 350 degrees F and put some oil on the casserole dish.
2. Cook chicken in hot oil for a few minutes.
3. Blend roasted red peppers in a blender before mixing these peppers, cooked chicken, garlic, mushrooms, tomatoes and onion in the prepared casserole dish.
4. Add salt, pepper, olive oil and on top of all this, put mozzarella cheese.
5. Bake in the preheated oven for about 30 minutes or until the cheese is melted.
6. Serve.

Dondurma (Turkish Ice Cream)

 Prep Time: 10 mins
 Total Time: 7 hr 30 mins

Servings per Recipe: 8
Calories   413 kcal
Carbohydrates   54.4 g
Cholesterol   218 mg
Fat   20.7 g
Fiber   0 g
Protein   4.6 g
Sodium   44 mg

Ingredients
- 1 1/2 cups water
- 2 cups white sugar
- 1 1/2 cups heavy cream
- 1 1/2 cups milk
- 6 egg yolks
- 3 tbsps instant coffee granules
- 2 tbsps finely ground coffee (optional)

Directions
1. Bring a mixture of water and sugar to boil until you see that the sugar has completely before adding this, cream and milk into a double boiler.
2. When completely mixed; add egg yolks and instant coffee.
3. Set the boiler over a pan containing hot water before cooking it for another ten minutes.
4. Pour this into a bowl using mesh strainer and add coffee grounds before refrigerating it for one full hour.
5. Pour this mixture into an ice cream maker and freeze it according to the directions of manufacturer.

BREAKFAST
Eggs in Turkey

🥣 Prep Time: 15 mins
🕐 Total Time: 20 mins

Servings per Recipe: 2
Calories   442 kcal
Carbohydrates   16.2 g
Cholesterol   600 mg
Fat   29.4 g
Fiber   0.5 g
Protein   29.1 g
Sodium   1599 mg

Ingredients
3 cloves garlic, peeled and minced
1 1/2 cups plain yogurt
1 pinch salt
1 quart water
1 tbsp vinegar
1 tsp salt
6 eggs
2 tbsps butter
1 tsp paprika

Directions
1. Mix garlic, salt and yoghurt in a small bowl.
2. Bring the mixture of water, salt and vinegar to boil over high heat before turning the heat down and adding eggs into the pan.
3. When the eggs are set; Transfer them to a serving platter.
4. Put yoghurt over these eggs and on top of all this, add mixture of melted butter and some paprika.
5. Serve.

A Turkish Soup of Red Lentils

Prep Time: 10 mins
Total Time: 1 hr 25 mins

Servings per Recipe: 6
Calories	442 kcal
Carbohydrates	64.2 g
Cholesterol	31 mg
Fat	14 g
Fiber	15.1 g
Protein	18.7 g
Sodium	1080 mg

Ingredients

- 1/4 cup butter
- 2 onions, finely chopped
- 1 tsp paprika
- 1 cup red lentils
- 1/2 cup fine bulgur
- 2 tbsps tomato paste
- 8 cups vegetable stock
- 1/8 tsp cayenne pepper
- 1 tbsp dried mint leaves
- 4 slices lemon
- 1/2 tsp chopped fresh mint

Directions

1. Cook onion in hot butter for about 15 minutes before adding paprika, bulgur and lentil into it.
2. Bring the mixture to boil after adding cayenne pepper, tomato sauce and vegetable stock into the pan, and cook all this for one full hour.
3. Stir in some mint leaves before turning the heat off and pouring the soup in reasonable bowls.
4. Garnish with some lemon slices and fresh mint before serving.

CLASSICAL
Turkish Greens

 Prep Time: 10 mins
Total Time: 20 mins

Servings per Recipe: 2
Calories   328 kcal
Carbohydrates   49.4 g
Cholesterol   17 mg
Fat   7 g
Fiber   10.2 g
Protein   6.7 g
Sodium   260 mg

Ingredients
2 cups beet greens
7 dried Turkish figs, stemmed and quartered
1/2 cup broth
2 cups fresh spinach
1 clove garlic, minced
2 tsps butter
salt to taste
1/2 ounce grated Parmesan cheese
(optional)

Directions
1. Cook beet greens, broth and figs over medium in a pan for about seven minutes before adding butter, spinach and garlic.
2. Turn the heat down to low and cook for another three minutes before adding some salt.
3. Put some parmesan cheese on top of all these vegetables before serving.

Manti (Turkish Ravioli)

Prep Time: 10 mins
Total Time: 20 mins

Servings per Recipe: 4	
Calories	293 kcal
Carbohydrates	26.7 g
Cholesterol	60 mg
Fat	17.1 g
Fiber	2.5 g
Protein	9.4 g
Sodium	1098 mg

Ingredients
1 tsp salt
1 tsp dried mint
1 (9 ounce) package beef ravioli
1/4 cup butter
1 tsp sweet paprika
1 tbsp minced garlic
1 (8 ounce) container plain whole milk yogurt

Directions
1. Cook salt, ravioli and mint in boiling water for five minutes before draining it.
2. Melt butter over a pan and add paprika before setting it aside to cool down.
3. Put yoghurt and garlic mixture over ravioli before adding that melted on top of all this.
4. Serve.

TURKISH
Cookies

Prep Time: 10 mins
Total Time: 20 mins

Servings per Recipe: 18
Calories   551 kcal
Carbohydrates   61 g
Cholesterol   112 mg
Fat   32 g
Fiber   1.3 g
Protein   5.7 g
Sodium   235 mg

Ingredients

2 cups all-purpose flour
1 cup butter, softened
1 cup confectioners' sugar
1 egg
1 tsp vanilla extract
1/4 cup strawberry preserves

Directions

1. Combine flour, butter or margarine, confectioners' sugar, egg and vanilla in a bowl very thoroughly before making 1.5 inch round doughs from it.
2. Place these on the baking sheet before making some place in the dough and placing jam.
3. Bake this at 350 degrees F for about twelve minutes or until you see that the bottoms are lightly brown.

A Turkish Inspired Ceviche

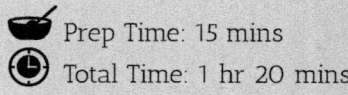

Prep Time: 15 mins
Total Time: 1 hr 20 mins

Servings per Recipe: 8
Calories	207 kcal
Carbohydrates	9.9 g
Cholesterol	129 mg
Fat	13 g
Fiber	2.5 g
Protein	16.2 g
Sodium	882 mg

Ingredients
- 1 lemon, halved and seeded
- 1 head garlic, halved
- 3 Turkish bay leaves
- 8 whole black peppercorns
- 1 tbsp kosher salt, or to taste
- 1 1/2 pounds peeled and deveined large shrimp (21 to 25 per lb)
- 2 cups coconut milk
- 1/2 cup lime juice
- 2 serrano chile peppers, thinly sliced
- 1/2 bunch cilantro, chopped
- 1 red onion, thinly sliced
- 8 sprigs cilantro, for garnish
- 1 lime, cut into 8 wedges

Directions
1. Bring a mixture of garlic, salt, squeezed lemon and its juice, bay leaves, water and peppercorns to boil over high heat before adding shrimp and turning the heat off.
2. Let it stand as it is for five minutes.
3. Drain this using a colander before letting it cool down for thirty minutes in baking dish.
4. Add shrimp that is cut in half lengthwise into the mixture of coconut milk, serrano peppers, chopped cilantro, lime juice and onion before refrigerating it for 30 minutes.
5. Garnish with lime wedges and cilantro sprigs before serving.

KISIR
(A Turkish Bulgur and Vegetable Salad)

 Prep Time: 15 mins
Total Time: 40 mins

Servings per Recipe: 6
Calories 216 kcal
Carbohydrates 30.4 g
Cholesterol 0 mg
Fat 9.8 g
Fiber 7.7 g
Protein 5.3 g
Sodium 19 mg

Ingredients

1 cup fine bulgur
1 cup boiling water
2 tbsps olive oil
1 onion, finely chopped
2 large tomatoes, finely chopped
1 cucumber, diced
2 green bell peppers, finely chopped
1 red bell peppers, finely chopped
7 green onions, finely chopped
1/2 cup minced fresh parsley
1/2 cup minced fresh mint leaves

1 tsp red pepper flakes, or to taste
2 tbsps olive oil
juice of 1 fresh lemon
2 tbsps pomegranate molasses

Directions

1. Let the bulgur stand in boiling water for twenty minutes.
2. In that time, cook onion in hot oil for about five minutes.
3. Mix bulgur, mint, cooked onion, cucumber, green and red bell peppers, chopped tomatoes, green onions, olive oil, pomegranate molasses, parsley, lemon juice and red pepper flakes in a bowl very thoroughly before serving.

Classical Bulgur

🥣 Prep Time: 15 mins
🕐 Total Time: 1 hr

Servings per Recipe: 6
Calories   323 kcal
Carbohydrates   53.1 g
Cholesterol   0 mg
Fat   8.1 g
Fiber   14.9 g
Protein   12.8 g
Sodium   511 mg

Ingredients

3 tbsps olive oil
1 onion, minced
1 ripe tomato, cut into small cubes
3 cups beef broth
2 cups bulgur, rinsed
salt and ground black pepper, or to taste
1/2 cup cooked green lentils
1/3 cup cooked chickpeas
1 bunch fresh mint, chopped

Directions

1. Cook onion in hot oil for about three minutes before adding tomatoes and cooking it for another two minutes.
2. Add beef broth into this pan before bring all this to boil.
3. Now put bulgur, black pepper and salt into the mixture, and cook all this for five minutes before adding lentils and chickpeas, and cooking all this for another five minutes or until you see that the bulgur is tender.
4. Let it cool down for 30 minutes before adding some mint for the purpose of serving.

TAVA II
(Turkish Stew)

Prep Time: 20 mins
Total Time: 1 hr 50 mins

Servings per Recipe: 8
Calories	316 kcal
Carbohydrates	29 g
Cholesterol	59 mg
Fat	13.7 g
Fiber	4.7 g
Protein	20.4 g
Sodium	823 mg

Ingredients
- 2 tbsps olive oil, divided
- 8 boneless chicken thighs, with skin
- 1 (6 ounce) can tomato paste
- 1/4 cup water
- 8 cloves garlic, halved
- salt and pepper to taste
- 4 medium potatoes, sliced
- 4 tomatoes, sliced
- 1 large onion, sliced
- 1 cup fresh mushrooms, sliced
- 8 pepperoncini peppers (optional)

Directions
1. Preheat your oven to 350 degrees F and put some oil over the quiche dish.
2. On top of chicken thighs in a baking dish containing some olive oil; add tomato sauce, pepper, potatoes, pepperoncini, tomatoes, mushrooms and onions before pouring the remaining olive oil over all this.
3. Bake in the preheated oven for about 90 minutes or until you see that the vegetables are tender.

Iskender Kebabs

🥣 Prep Time: 15 mins
⏱ Total Time: 30 mins

Servings per Recipe: 4
Calories   667 kcal
Carbohydrates   48.6 g
Cholesterol   144 mg
Fat   36.2 g
Fiber   3.9 g
Protein   37.3 g
Sodium   886 mg

Ingredients

- 4 pita bread rounds
- 1 tbsp olive oil
- 4 skinless, boneless chicken breast halves - chopped
- 2 medium onion, chopped
- 1 clove garlic, minced
- 1 (10.75 ounce) can tomato puree
- ground cumin to taste
- salt to taste
- ground black pepper to taste
- 1/2 cup butter, melted
- 1 cup Greek yogurt
- 1/4 cup chopped fresh parsley

Directions

1. Preheat your oven to 350 degrees F and bake pita bread in it for some time before cutting it down into small pieces.
2. Cook garlic, chicken and onion in hot oil for some time before adding tomato puree, pepper, salt and cumin, and cooking it for another ten minutes.
3. On top of pita bread in a serving platter; put chicken mixture and some butter.
4. Garnish with some parsley and yoghurt before you serve it.

MOUSSAKA
(Potato Casserole from the Ottoman Empire)

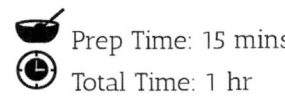

Prep Time: 15 mins
Total Time: 1 hr

Servings per Recipe: 5
Calories	728 kcal
Carbohydrates	44.3 g
Cholesterol	145 mg
Fat	49.4 g
Fiber	6.2 g
Protein	27.8 g
Sodium	961 mg

Ingredients
5 tbsps olive oil
1 pound ground beef
1 tsp ground paprika
1 tsp ground cumin
1 tsp salt
1 tsp ground black pepper
4 potatoes, peeled and cut into 1/2-inch cubes
1 (6.5 ounce) can tomato sauce
1 tbsp chopped summer savory (chubritsa)
1 egg, lightly beaten

2/3 cup yogurt

Directions
1. Preheat your oven to 325 degrees F.
2. Cook ground beef in hot oil until you see that it is brown from all sides before adding paprika, pepper, cumin, tomatoes and salt into it, and cooking it for another three minutes.
3. After turning the heat down to low and adding tomato sauce; cook all this for 15 more minutes.
4. Now pour the mixture of egg and yoghurt over this meat mixture in the baking dish.
5. Bake in the preheated oven for about 40 minutes or until the top is golden brown in color.

Dukkah (Levantine Spice Mix)

Prep Time: 20 mins
Total Time: 25 mins

Servings per Recipe: 2
Calories   45 kcal
Carbohydrates   2.1 g
Cholesterol   0 mg
Fat   4 g
Fiber   1.1 g
Protein   1.3 g
Sodium   75 mg

Ingredients
2/3 cup hazelnuts
1/2 cup sesame seeds
2 tbsps coriander seeds
2 tbsps cumin seeds
2 tbsps freshly ground black pepper
1 tsp flaked sea salt

Directions
1. Remove the skin from hazelnuts by rubbing after baking in a preheated oven at 350 degrees for five minutes.
2. Toast sesame seeds, coriander and cumin seeds separately in a pan until golden brown before placing them in the blender.
3. Blend them one by one, so that the end product is smooth.
4. Add hazelnuts in the blender and blend all the content until you see that everything is finely crushed.
5. Transfer to a bowl and mix it well with spices, and season with salt and pepper according to your taste.
6. Serve.

CLASSICAL
Turkish Chevre

Prep Time: 10 mins
Total Time: 2 hr 40 mins

Servings per Recipe: 8
Calories 96 kcal
Carbohydrates 1.7 g
Cholesterol 18 mg
Fat 7.6 g
Fiber 0.7 g
Protein 5 g
Sodium 119 mg

Ingredients

1 (8 ounce) log of fresh goat cheese (chevre)
1/2 tsp Urfa biber, or to taste
2 tbsps finely crushed cocoa nibs

Directions

1. Mix urfa biber and goat cheese (that has been placed at room temperature for about 30 minutes) in a bowl before wrapping it around a plastic to get it into log shape by placing it in the freezer for about one hour.
2. Coat cocoa nibs very thorough with this cheese before wrapping it up again to be chilled for one more hour.
3. Serve this after bringing this to room temperature.

Shakshouka (Levantine Spicy Eggs)

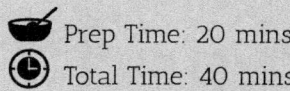

Prep Time: 20 mins
Total Time: 40 mins

Servings per Recipe:	4
Calories	209 kcal
Carbohydrates	12.9 g
Cholesterol	164 mg
Fat	15 g
Fiber	3.1 g
Protein	7.8 g
Sodium	654 mg

Ingredients

- 3 tbsps olive oil
- 1 1/3 cups chopped onion
- 1 cup thinly sliced bell peppers, any color
- 2 cloves garlic, minced, or to taste
- 2 1/2 cups chopped tomatoes
- 1 tsp ground cumin
- 1 tsp paprika
- 1 tsp salt
- 1 hot chile pepper, seeded and finely chopped, or to taste
- 4 eggs

Directions

1. Cook onion, garlic and bell peppers in hot oil for about five minutes or until you see that the vegetables have softened up.
2. Add the mixture of chili pepper, tomatoes, salt, cumin and paprika into this pan before cooking it for another ten minutes.
3. Make space for eggs in the mixture and cook these eggs by covering the pan, and cooking it for five minutes or until the eggs are firm.
4. Serve.

DOLMAS
(Stuffed Grape Leaves)

Prep Time: 30 mins
Total Time: 1 hr 15 mins

Servings per Recipe: 8
Calories   207 kcal
Carbohydrates   39.1 g
Cholesterol   0 mg
Fat   3.8 g
Fiber   2 g
Protein   5.3 g
Sodium   847 mg

Ingredients
1 tbsp olive oil
2 onions, minced
1 1/2 cups uncooked white rice
2 tbsps tomato paste
2 tbsps dried currants
2 tbsps pine nuts
1 tbsp ground cinnamon
1 tbsp dried mint
1 tbsp dried dill weed
1 tsp ground allspice
1 tsp ground cumin
1 (8 ounce) jar grape leaves, drained and rinsed

Directions
1. Cook onion in hot oil until tender before adding rice and hot water, and cooking all this for ten minutes or until the rice is cooked.
2. Turn the heat off and stir in tomato paste, allspice, currants, mint leaves, pine nuts, cinnamon, dill weed, allspice and cumin.
3. Place rinse grape leaves in warm water before cutting the stems and filling the center of leaf with cooked rice.
4. Fold it up and place in the pot having inverted plate at the bottom.
5. Add enough water to cover the dolmas and cook it over low heat for about 45 minutes.
6. Serve.

Mediterranean Kofta

🍲 Prep Time: 15 mins
🕒 Total Time: 35 mins

Servings per Recipe: 4
Calories 482.3
Fat 32.8g
Cholesterol 129.6mg
Sodium 576.2mg
Carbohydrates 20.8g
Protein 24.3g

Ingredients

- 1 C fine fresh breadcrumb
- 1 lb lean ground lamb
- 1/2 tsp salt
- 1/2 tsp pepper
- 1 tsp ground cumin
- 1/2 tsp allspice
- 1 tsp dried mint
- 2 cloves garlic
- 2 tbsp parsley
- 1 egg
- 1 tbsp olive oil

Directions

1. Cut to pieces of whole wheat bread that is not all dried out and place them in a blender.
2. Pulse them several times until turn into crumbs. Combine in the garlic with parsley and spices them then process them several times again until they are well combined.
3. Transfer the mix to a mixing bowl and start shaping it into bite size meatballs.
4. Place a large pan over medium heat and heat the oil in it.
5. Add the meatballs gradually in batches then cook them until they become brown.
6. Remove the patties from the hot oil and pan and drain them then serve them warm with your favorite toppings.
7. Enjoy.

HOT YOGURT
Chicken Thighs

Prep Time: 15 mins
Total Time: 1 hr 45 mins

Servings per Recipe: 4
Calories 144.1
Fat 4.3g
Cholesterol 71.7mg
Sodium 405.9mg
Carbohydrates 6.0g
Protein 19.6g

Ingredients
8 bone-in skinless chicken thighs
1 tbsp lemon juice
1 C plain low-fat yogurt
2 garlic cloves (minced)
1 tbsp fresh ginger (minced)
2 tsp hot paprika
1 1/2 tsp dried mint
1/2 tsp salt

Directions
1. Stir the chicken thighs with lemon juice in a large mixing bowl.
2. Mix the yogurt, garlic, ginger, paprika, mint, and salt in a small mixing bowl.
3. Spoon the mix to the lemon chicken thighs and combine them well.
4. Cover the bowl and place it in the fridge to marinate for 1 h 30 min to 24 h.
5. Before you do anything preheat the oven broiler.
6. Drain the chicken thighs from the marinade and place them in the oven broiler. Cook them for 17 min.
7. Before you do anything else, lower the heat temperature of the oven to 400 f.
8. Place it in the chicken thighs and cook them for another 17 min. serve them hot.
9. Enjoy.

Saucy Turkish Burger Meatloaf

Prep Time: 30 mins
Total Time: 3 hr 30 mins

Servings per Recipe: 1
Calories   1983.8
Fat   79.8g
Cholesterol   477.1mg
Sodium   1464.7mg
Carbohydrates   159.6g
Protein   151.0g

Ingredients

Meatloaf:
3 lbs lean hamburger
3/4 C breadcrumbs
2 tsp pepper
1 - 2 tsp red cayenne pepper
1 1/2 tsp oregano
3 tsp paprika
2 tsp onion powder
1 tsp garlic powder
1/2 tsp salt

Sauce:
2/3 C canned milk
2/3 C sugar
2 tbsp white vinegar
1/2 tsp garlic powder

Sandwich:
pita bread
chopped onion
sliced tomatoes

Directions

1. To make the meatloaf:
2. Mix the burger meat with breadcrumbs, oregano, onion and garlic powder, paprika, and salt in a large mixing bowl.
3. Split the mix into half and shape each half into a loaf.
4. Before you do anything else preheat the oven broiler to 300 f.
5. Place the loaves on a lined up baking sheet then cook them in the oven broiler for 2 h to 35 min.
6. Place the meatloaves aside and let them lose heat until they become cool to the touch. Use a sharp knife to cut the meatloaves into thin slices and place them aside.
7. To make the sauce:
8. Whisk the canned milk, sugar and garlic powder in a small bowl until the sugar melt.
9. Add the vinegar gradually while mixing all the time. Place the sauce in the fridge for 1 h 20 min or more.
10. To make the sandwich:
11. Place a frying pan to heat over medium heat.
12. Drench pita bread in water then heat it in the pan.
13. Place on it some meatloaves slices followed by the onion, tomato then the sauce at last. Serve your pita bread meatloaves.
14. Enjoy.

FLAMING TURKISH
Yogurt and Chicken Kebabs

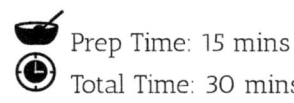

Prep Time: 15 mins
Total Time: 30 mins

Servings per Recipe: 6
Calories   435.9
Fat   32.8g
Cholesterol   143.2mg
Sodium   754.7mg
Carbohydrates   4.0g
Protein   30.1g

Ingredients
1 1/2 tbsp Aleppo pepper
1 C Greek yogurt
3 tbsp olive oil
2 tbsp red wine vinegar
2 tbsp tomato paste
2 tsp kosher salt
1 tsp black pepper
6 garlic cloves, minced
2 lemons (1-thinly sliced & 1 cut in wedges)
2 1/4 lbs chicken thighs (boneless, cut into 1 1/2-inch pieces)

Directions
1. Whisk the Aleppo pepper with 1 tbsp of warm water. Place the mix aside to soften for 6 min. stir the mix until well combined.
2. Mix the yogurt, olive oil, red wine vinegar, tomato paste, 2 tsp kosher salt and 1 tsp black pepper in a large mixing bowl to make the marinade.
3. Add the Aleppo pepper and lemon mix then combine the well followed by the lemon and garlic pieces.
4. Place 1/3 C of the mix aside for later use. Stir the chicken pieces into the rest of the marinade in the bowl then place it in the fridge for 28 min.
5. Before you do anything preheat the grill.
6. Drain the chicken pieces from the marinade and thread them into sewers.
7. Place the chicken kabobs on the grill and cook for 10 to 14 min for each one while basting them with the reserved 1/3 C of the marinade.
8. Serve your kabobs hot with your favorite sauce.
9. Enjoy.

Chicken Pilaf

Prep Time: 10 mins
Total Time: 50 mins

Servings per Recipe: 4
Calories   499.4
Fat   22.5g
Cholesterol   421.7mg
Sodium   791.3mg
Carbohydrates   49.2g
Protein   25.3g

Ingredients
- 1 lb chicken liver, washed and patted dry
- 4 tbsp butter
- 1 tsp salt
- Pepper
- 1 1/2 C thinly sliced scallions
- 2 medium tomatoes, peeled, seeded and chopped
- 2 tbsp pine nuts
- 2 tbsp chopped almonds
- 2 tbsp raisins
- 1 C uncooked white rice
- 2 tbsp chopped fresh parsley

Directions
1. Place a pan over medium heat and melt in it 2 tbsp of butter. Add the chicken livers and cook them for 6 min. stir in 1/2 tsp salt and pepper.
2. Place the mix aside. Stir half of the sliced scallions to the pan and cook them for 2 min then drain them and place them aside.
3. Place a large saucepan over medium heat and melt the rest of the butter in it. Add the rest of the scallions then cook them for 2 min.
4. Stir in the raisins with tomatoes and cook them for an extra 3 min. stir in the rice and cook them for 1 to 2 min.
5. Combine in 2 C water, 1/2 tsp salt and pepper then let cook until they start boiling over medium heat.
6. Low the heat then put on the lid and let the rice mix cook for 27 min with the lid on.
7. once the time is up, spread the cooked chicken liver mix on top followed by the half cooked scallions then put on the lid and cook them for 1 min to heat them.
8. Serve your chicken livers pilaf warm.
9. Enjoy.

MINTY
Potato Salad

Prep Time: 10 mins
Total Time: 35 mins

Servings per Recipe: 2
Calories   139.2
Fat   6.8g
Cholesterol   0.0mg
Sodium   152.7mg
Carbohydrates   17.7g
Protein   2.0g

Ingredients

200 g potatoes, peeled
1 tbsp olive oil
1 tbsp white vinegar
1 tsp dried mint
1/8 tsp salt, to taste
1/8 tsp ground black pepper, to taste

Directions

1. Slice the potatoes in small dices. Bring a salted pot of water to a boil then cook in it the potato until it becomes soft. Remove it from the water.
2. Toss the cooked potato with olive oil, white vinegar, dried mint, salt and black pepper. Place the salad in the fridge to lose heat for 1 h.
3. Enjoy.

Turkish Cheesy Spinach Pizza

Prep Time: 15 mins
Total Time: 40 mins

Servings per Recipe: 4
Calories 393.6
Fat 28.9g
Cholesterol 61.7mg
Sodium 520.9mg
Carbohydrates 19.5g
Protein 17.5g

Ingredients
1 pizza dough
1 tbsp butter
2 garlic cloves, crushed
1 bunch spinach, washed and shredded
4 scallions, thinly sliced
250 g fresh ricotta cheese
100 g feta cheese, crumbled
1/2 C pine nuts
1/2 C fresh breadcrumb
Olive oil flavored cooking spray
Lemon wedge, to serve

Directions
1. Place a large skillet over medium heat and heat the butter in it. Sauté in it the spinach with garlic for 40 sec.
2. Drain them and place them aside to lose heat. Combine in the scallions, ricotta, feta, pine nuts and breadcrumbs with a pinch of salt and pepper to make the filling.
3. Before you do anything preheat the oven to 400 f.
4. Slice the pizza dough into 4 pieces then roll them into a circular shape making 25 cm.
5. Split the spinach mix into the pizza dough then fold their sides slightly and bring each two of them to together in the middle in the shape of a boat.
6. Transfer the pizzas to line up baking trays then cook them for 28 min until they become golden brown. Serve them warm.
7. Enjoy.

CHERRY SAUCY
Lamb Kabobs with Cucumber Salad

Prep Time: 25 mins
Total Time: 40 mins

Servings per Recipe: 8
Calories   371.4
Fat   27.1g
Cholesterol   67.9mg
Sodium   81.3mg
Carbohydrates   13.2g
Protein   19.9g

Ingredients

2 lbs lamb, cubes about 1 inches each
2 green peppers
2 pints cherry tomatoes
2 onions
Marinade:
2 tbsp lemon juice
1/2 C olive oil
1 tsp garlic, minced
1/2 tsp cumin
1/4 tsp turmeric (or more if desired, depending on how spicy you desire)
1 pinch ground red pepper or 1 pinch cayenne
For the White Sauce:
2 cucumbers, peeled and grated
16 ozs cold plain yogurt
2 garlic cloves, minced
1 tbsp of fresh mint
Salt
Olive oil

Directions

1. Toss the cucumbers and garlic salt in a large mixing bowl. Stir in the yogurt then top it with the mint and some olive oil.
2. Put on the lid then place the salad in the fridge.
3. Grease the skewers with some oil or a cooking spray then thread into them the tomato, onion and lamb dices. Brush them once again with some oil.
4. Before you do anything preheat the grill.
5. Cook the skewers for 6 to 10 min while turning every once in a while. Serve your kabobs warm with the cucumber salad and some pita bread.
6. Enjoy.

Saucy Greens Potato Salad

Prep Time: 20 mins
Total Time: 45 mins

Servings per Recipe: 6
Calories 269.6
Fat 5.1g
Cholesterol 0.0mg
Sodium 238.9mg
Carbohydrates 52.4g
Protein 7.6g

Ingredients
- 3 onions cut into crescents
- 2 tbsp olive oil
- 1 1/2 lbs green beans
- 3 large ripe tomatoes cut into wedges
- 1 C tomato sauce
- 1 C water
- 3 large potatoes cut into chunks
- Salt and pepper

Directions
1. Place a skillet over medium heat and heat the oil in it.
2. Cook in it the onions for 3 to 5 min or until it becomes golden.
3. Stir in the rest of the ingredients then put on the lid and let them cook for 5 to 10 min or until they become soft.
4. Serve your warm veggies salad with your favorite toppings.
5. Enjoy.

SPICED-UP Lamb Stew

Prep Time: 5 mins
Total Time: 2 hr

Servings per Recipe: 3
Calories	328.0
Fat	17.9g
Cholesterol	108.5mg
Sodium	170.5mg
Carbohydrates	5.6g
Protein	34.6g

Ingredients
- 1/2 kg boneless stewing lamb
- 2 tbsp olive oil
- 1 medium onion, finely chopped
- 1 garlic clove, minced
- 1/4 C chopped sweet pepper (red, orange, yellow, or green) (optional)
- 1/2 C canned tomatoes, pureed or 3/4 C chopped peeled tomatoes
- 3/4 C water
- 1/2 tsp baharat, spice mix Baharat Spice Blend or 1/2 tsp ground allspice
- Salt
- Fresh ground black pepper
- 1/4 C chopped parsley

Directions
1. Place a large pan over medium heat and heat in it half of the oil. Cook in it the lamb meat until it becomes evenly brown.
2. Drain it and place it aside. Add the rest of the oil and heat it. Sauté in it the onion, garlic and sweet pepper for 4 to 6 min. stir in the water with tomato.
3. Mix in the bahrat or allspice, salt and pepper to taste and most of the parsley.
4. Stir in the meat back then put on the lid and cook them for 1 h 30 min. once the stew sauce becomes thick, serve it hot with some rice.
5. Enjoy.

Baharat Spice Mix at Home

Prep Time: 5 mins
Total Time: 5 mins

Servings per Recipe: 1
Calories   187.5
Fat   8.3 g
Cholesterol   0.0 mg
Sodium   46.0 mg
Carbohydrates   35.2 g
Protein   6.7 g

Ingredients
4 tbsp ground black pepper
2 tbsp ground coriander
2 tbsp ground cinnamon
2 tbsp ground cloves
3 tbsp ground cumin
1 tsp ground cardamom
4 tsp ground nutmeg
4 tbsp paprika

Directions
1. In a bowl, add all the ingredients and mix well.
2. Transfer the mixture into a glass jar and seal tightly.
3. Store in a cool, dry place.

MINTY FETA and Courgette Patties

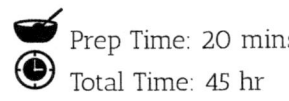
Prep Time: 20 mins
Total Time: 45 hr

Servings per Recipe: 4
Calories   333.5
Fat   24.8g
Cholesterol   203.1mg
Sodium   624.3mg
Carbohydrates   14.6g
Protein   14.2g

Ingredients
1 large onion, chopped coarsely
3 tbsp sunflower oil
500 g courgettes, chopped finely
3 eggs
3 tbsp plain flour
2 sprigs of fresh mint, chopped
2 sprigs fresh dill, chopped
200 g feta cheese, mashed with a fork
Oil (for frying)

Directions
1. Place a large skillet over medium heat and heat 3 tbsp of oil in it. Cook in it the onion until it becomes golden and soft.
2. Stir in the courgettes and cook them until they are done.
3. Whisk the eggs with flour. Stir in the black pepper with herbs. Add the feta cheese and stir them gently followed by the onion and courgettes mix.
4. Grease a large skillet with some oil and heat it over medium heat.
5. Shape the mix into small patties using a tbsp then place them in the heated skillet. Coo them until they become golden brown on both sides.
6. Serve your courgette patties warm with your favorite toppings and enjoy.

Hot Lamb Kabobs with Bloody Mary Hummus

Prep Time: 30 mins
Total Time: 40 mins

Servings per Recipe: 2
Calories   648.4
Fat   45.3g
Cholesterol   117.2mg
Sodium   1111.9mg
Carbohydrates   23.5g
Protein   38.0g

Ingredients

- 350 g leg of lamb, fat trimmed
- 1 bell pepper, cut into chunks (any color)
- 1 red onion, half cut into chunks, half sliced
- 100 g white mushrooms
- 3 tbsp olive oil
- 1 cooked beetroot
- 75 g chickpeas, rinsed and drained (can)
- 1/2 lemon, juiced
- 1/2 tsp tahini
- 2 garlic cloves, crushed
- 1 tbsp harissa
- 1 tsp dried oregano
- 2 sprigs fresh rosemary, finely chopped
- 3/4 tsp himalayan pink salt

Directions

1. To make the kabobs:
2. Cut the lamb meat into small dices.
3. Mix the sliced onion, 1 clove of garlic, harissa paste, oregano, rosemary and 1 tbsp of olive oil in a large mixing bowl to make the marinade.
4. Season the lamb pieces with some salt then stir them into the marinade. Place the kabobs in the fridge to marinate for 1 h.
5. To make the hummus:
6. Combine the beetroot, chickpeas, tahini, 2 tbsp of olive oil, 1/4 tsp salt, and 1 clove of garlic and lemon juice in a food processor then process until they become smooth.
7. Place the hummus aside until ready to serve.
8. Place the mushrooms with pieces of pepper, onion and lamb pieces into skewers.
9. Before you do anything preheat the grill and grease its grates. Cook in it the skewers for 3 to 5 min on each side. Once the time is up, serve your kabobs warm with hummus.
10. Enjoy.

MINTY Beef Sandwiches

Prep Time: 10 mins
Total Time: 25 mins

Servings per Recipe: 4
Calories 206.4
Fat 3.9g
Cholesterol 13.4mg
Sodium 781.3mg
Carbohydrates 34.3g
Protein 7.7g

Ingredients

1 1/2 lbs lean ground beef
1/2 tsp salt
1/4 tsp pepper
1/4 tsp cumin
2 oz feta cheese, cut into 4 cubes
2 tbsp of fresh mint, chopped
4 pita breads (or 2 large ones cut in half)
OPTIONAL CONDIMENTS
Hummus
Cucumber, thinly sliced
Red onion, thinly sliced

Fresh tomato, sliced
Fresh basil leaf
Fresh spinach leaves

Directions

1. Mix the beef, salt, pepper and cumin. Shape the mix into 4 pieces and place them aside.
2. Place the feta dices on a working surface and press them until they become flat then top them with the mint.
3. Flatten a piece of the beef mix on your hands slightly then place the feta piece in the middle then wrap the meat mix around it shaping it into a burger.
4. Repeat the process with the rest of the ingredients. Place a large skillet over medium heat and heat some oil in it.
5. Cook the patties in the hot pan for 6 to 8 min on each side. Once the time is up, serve your patties in the pita breads with your favorite toppings.
6. Enjoy.

Mediterranean Omelets

Prep Time: 10 mins
Total Time: 25 mins

Servings per Recipe: 4
Calories	243.5
Fat	11.9g
Cholesterol	475.8mg
Sodium	184.4mg
Carbohydrates	18.2g
Protein	17.6g

Ingredients
- 9 eggs
- 200 g onions, sliced
- 1 bunch fresh parsley, chopped
- 300 g green peppers, diced
- 6 tomatoes, chopped
- Butter, to taste
- Salt, to taste

Directions
1. Beat the eggs in a mixing bowl. Season it with some salt.
2. Place a skillet over medium heat and melt the butter in it. Cook in it the pepper with onion, salt and tomato for 5 min.
3. Spread the veggies in the pan and pour the eggs all over them. Serve your omelets with the parsley on top and your favorite other toppings.
4. Enjoy.

FETA
Chicken Pizza

 Prep Time: 20 mins
Total Time: 1 hr

Servings per Recipe: 6
Calories   265.9
Fat   11.1g
Cholesterol   75.2mg
Sodium   710.9mg
Carbohydrates   15.6g
Protein   28.6g

Ingredients
2 skinless chicken breasts
1/3 C lemon juice
1 tbsp olive oil
2 cloves garlic, crushed
1/3 C of fresh mint, chopped
1 medium onion, chopped
1 (425 g) cans crushed tomatoes
1 kg English spinach
2 Turkish bread (44cm)
200 g reduced fat feta cheese

Directions
1. Toss the chicken with lemon juice, oil, garlic and half the mint in a large mixing bowl. Place it in the fridge covered for 3 h.
2. Once the time is up, drain the chicken and place it aside then reserve the marinade aside.
3. Place a non-sticking pan of medium heat and heat it then brown in it the chicken breasts on both sides. Place them aside to lose heat for a while.
4. Cut the chicken breasts into slices. Pour the reserved marinade into the same pan and heat it.
5. Stir in the onion and cook it for 3 to 6 min or until it becomes soft.
6. Stir in the tomato and cook them for 12 min over low heat until the mix becomes thick.
7. Bring the mix to a boil. Steam or microwave the spinach until the soften and welt then press them with your hands to remove the excess water.
8. Place the Turkish bread on a lined up baking sheet spread on them the tomato mix followed by the chicken, spinach, feta and mint.
9. Preheat the oven. Cook in it the Turkish pizza for 22 min. serve them warm.
10. Enjoy.

Karniyarik (Turkish Eggplants)

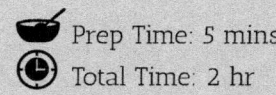 Prep Time: 5 mins
Total Time: 2 hr

Servings per Recipe: 6
Calories 288.3
Fat 10.9g
Cholesterol 44.4mg
Sodium 188.5mg
Carbohydrates 35.0g
Protein 18.1g

Ingredients

6 thin and long medium-size eggplants
Salt
Sunflower oil, for frying
2 onions, chopped
14 oz ground beef or 14 oz lamb
1 tbsp tomato paste
2 large tomatoes
1 tsp ground cinnamon
1/2 tsp ground allspice
Black pepper
1/3 C chopped flat leaf parsley
1 C tomato juice

Directions

1. Take of the eggplant caps while leaving the stems on then peel them by removing wide stripes leaving some of the skin in the process.
2. Fill a large bowl with water and 1 tbsp of salt then place in it the eggplants for 32 min.
3. Remove them from the water and pat them dry.
4. Place a large skillet over medium heat and heat some oil in it then cook it in the eggplants until they become slightly golden brown on each side.
5. Place another skillet over medium heat and heat 3 tbsp of oil in it. Add the onion and cook it for 4 min.
6. Stir in the meat and cook them for another 6 min. stir in the tomato paste with 1 chopped tomato, cinnamon, allspice, salt, pepper, and chopped parsley.
7. Cook them for 12 min over low heat while stirring all the time.
8. Before you do anything preheat the oven to 350 f.
9. Lay the browned eggplants in a greased casserole dish.
10. Use a sharp knife to make a slit in the belly of each eggplant without cutting completely then use a spoon to press it inside and make it hollow.
11. Spoon the meaty tomato mix into the slit of each eggplant then cut the remaining tomato into slices and places them on top.
12. Drizzle the tomato juice on top then place a piece of foil on top to cover them.
13. Cook the meaty eggplant casserole dish for 42 min then serve it warm.
14. Enjoy.

TZATZIKI
Steak Kabobs

Prep Time: 40 mins
Total Time: 1 d 50 mins

Servings per Recipe: 6
Calories   512 kcal
Fat   34.3 g
Carbohydrates   36 g
Protein   15.7 g
Cholesterol   33 mg
Sodium   891 mg

Ingredients

Marinade:
- 2 large onions, chopped
- 2 garlic cloves, crushed
- 1/2 C olive oil
- 2 tbsp lemon juice
- 1 tsp dried oregano
- 1 tsp ground black pepper
- 1/2 tsp ground turmeric
- 1 pinch curry powder
- 1 tsp salt
- 1 lb beef flank steak, thinly sliced

Tzatziki Sauce:
- 8 oz sour cream
- 2 tbsp olive oil
- 1 tbsp lemon juice
- 1/2 tsp salt
- 1/2 tsp ground black pepper
- 1 tbsp chopped fresh dill
- 1 clove garlic, crushed
- 6 pita bread rounds

Directions

1. Put the onion in a mixing bowl then press it with a glass to get the excess water out from it.
2. add the 2 crushed garlic cloves, 1/2 C olive oil, 2 tbsp lemon juice, oregano, 1 tsp black pepper, turmeric, curry powder, and 1 tsp salt then combine them well.
3. Combine in the beef slices then put on a lid of a piece of plastic and place it in the fridge for 12 h.
4. Whisk the sour cream, 2 tbsp olive oil, 1 tbsp lemon juice, 1/2 tsp salt, 1/2 tsp black pepper, dill, and 1 crushed clove of garlic in a mixing bowl.
5. Cover it with a piece of plastic and place it in the fridge for 12 h to make the sauce.
6. Before you do anything preheat the oven broiler. Please the 6 rack inches away from the heat.
7. Drain the beef slices from the marinade and lay them on a greased baking sheet then season them with a pinch of salt.
8. Cook them in the oven for 6 min while flipping them halfway through time. Transfer the meat slices into the pita breads and top them with the cream sauce then serve them warm.
9. Enjoy.

Turkish Small Burgers

Prep Time: 30 mins
Total Time: 1 hr 40 min

Servings per Recipe: 6
Calories	381 kcal
Fat	25.1 g
Carbohydrates	9.9 g
Protein	28.2 g
Cholesterol	142 mg
Sodium	548 mg

Ingredients

- 1 lb ground lamb
- 1 lb ground beef
- 1 tsp salt
- 1 tsp ground black pepper
- 1 tbsp ground cumin
- 2 tsp ground sweet paprika
- 3 tbsp tomato paste
- 2 onions, peeled and cut into chunks
- 4 cloves garlic, peeled
- 1 tbsp olive oil
- 1/4 bunch fresh parsley, chopped
- 3 tbsp all-purpose flour
- 2 small eggs

Directions

1. Place the lamb, beef, salt, pepper, cumin, paprika, and tomato paste in a large mixing bowl without combining them and put it aside.
2. Get a food processor: combine in the garlic with onion and process them while adding the olive oil gradually. Combine in the parsley and process them again.
3. Add the parsley mix to the meats mix and combine them well with your hands. Add the eggs with flour and mix them again with your hands. Place the mix aside to rest for 6 min.
4. Mix them again and shape the mix into several medium sized burgers. Place them on a baking sheet, cover them with a piece of plastic and place them in the fridge for 1 h.
5. Before you do anything preheat the oven broiler and put the rack 3 inches away from the heat.
6. Place the burgers on a foil lined up baking sheet and cook them in the oven until they become golden brown on both sides. Serve them warm with your favorite toppings.
7. Enjoy.

MINTY LAMB
Pizza with Garlic Cream Sauce

 Prep Time: 2 h
Total Time: 1 d 3 h 20 m

Servings per Recipe: 10
Calories   480 kcal
Fat   20.1 g
Carbohydrates   57.6 g
Protein   17.2 g
Cholesterol   35 mg
Sodium   571 mg

Ingredients

For the Lamb Sauce:
1 tsp chopped garlic
1 yellow onion, chopped
3 tbsp chopped fresh basil
1/2 C chopped fresh parsley
2 tbsp chopped fresh mint
1/2 tsp paprika
1/2 tsp ground cumin
1/2 tsp ground coriander seed
1/2 C green bell pepper, diced
1/2 C red bell pepper, diced
1/2 lemon, juiced
4 tsp olive oil
4 roma (plum) tomatoes, halved
1 lb lean ground lamb
6 tbsp double concentrated tomato paste
Cayenne pepper to taste
Salt to taste

For the Dough:
3 1/4 tsp active dry yeast
1/2 tsp white sugar
1 C warm water (110 degrees F/45 degrees C)
5 C all-purpose flour
2 tsp salt
1/4 C vegetable oil
1/2 C water

For the Garlic Sauce:
1 C plain yogurt
1/2 tsp chopped fresh parsley
1/4 tsp crushed garlic
Salt and ground black pepper to taste

For the Garnish:
1 C shredded green cabbage
1 C shredded red cabbage

Directions

1. Place a large pan over medium heat. Brown in it the lamb
2. Get a food processor: add to it the garlic, onion, basil, parsley, mint, paprika, cumin, coriander, diced bell peppers, lemon juice, tomatoes, and olive oil.
3. Process them until they become smooth. Stir in the tomato mix with tomato paste and cook them for 16 min until they become thick while stirring all the time.
4. Add the pinch of salt with cayenne pepper and turn off the heat. Pour the mix into a casserole dish and place it aside to lose heat.
5. Cover it and place it in the fridge for 12 h.
6. Stir the sugar with yeast and 1 C of warm water. Mix the salt with flour in a large mixing bowl.
7. Stir the vegetable oil and 1/2 C water into the sugar and yeast water mix. Add the mix to the flour and mix them well with your hands.

8. Sprinkle some flour on a working surface and keep pulling it with your hands until it softens for 9 min.
9. Get a large bowl: grease it with some vegetable oil and place the dough on it. Cover it with a piece of plastic and place it aside to rise for 1 h.
10. Place the meaty tomato sauce aside to adjust to the kitchen temperature.
11. To make the creamy garlic sauce:
12. Stir the yogurt, parsley, crushed garlic, and salt and pepper. Place it in the fridge until ready to serve.
13. Before you do anything preheat the oven to 500 f.
14. Sprinkle some flour on a working surface and place the dough on it. Cut it into 10 pieces and roll each one into a circular shape.
15. Place the dough circles on a lined up baking sheet. Spread on each one of them the meaty tomato sauce. Cook the pizzas in the oven for 6 to 10 min until they become golden.
16. Place the pizzas on serving plates then top them with the garlic sauce and some shredded cabbage.
17. Enjoy.

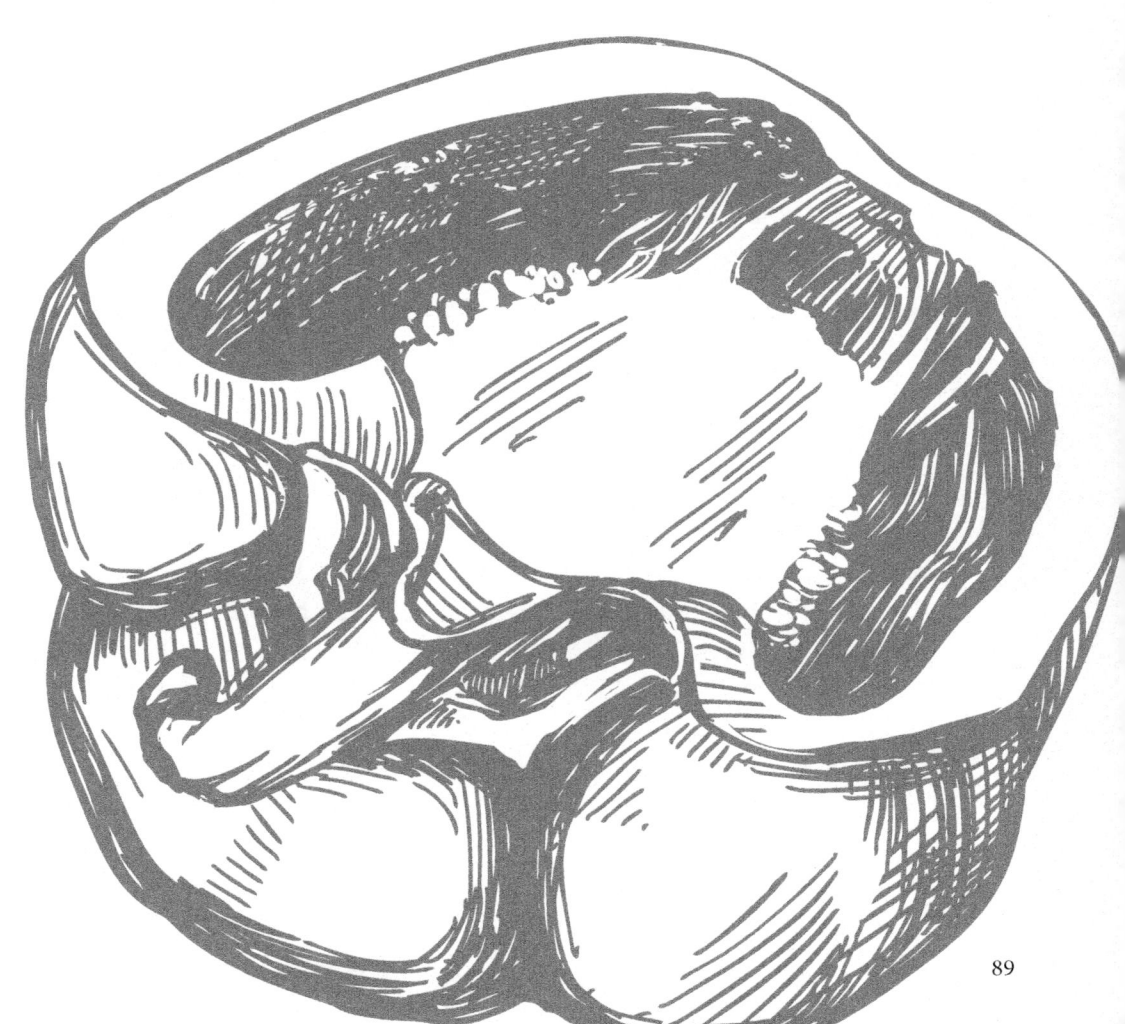

GOLDEN Shrimp Bites

🥣 Prep Time: 10 mins
🕐 Total Time: 20 mins

Servings per Recipe: 4
Calories   494.9
Fat   40.3g
Cholesterol   166.2mg
Sodium   646.0mg
Carbohydrates   16.5g
Protein   17.0g

Ingredients
6 oz shrimp, cut in half
2 tbsp butter
3 tbsp flour
1/2 C milk
1/2 C mozzarella cheese, grated
1/2 tsp salt
1/2 tsp pepper
1 tbsp lemon juice
1 egg, lightly beaten, with
1/2 tsp olive oil
1/2 C breadcrumbs

FOR FRYING
1/2 C sunflower oil

Directions
1. Place a large saucepan over medium heat then heat the butter in it. Combine in the flour and mix them well.
2. Add the milk gradually while whisking all the time until you get a smooth mix that is free of lumps.
3. Combine in the cheese, shrimp, lemon juice, salt and pepper then cook them for 4 min.
4. Transfer the mix to a mixing bowl and place it in the fridge to lose heat.
5. Spread some flour on a working space on a counter then dump in it the shrimp mix. Shape the mix into small patties.
6. Dip each patty in the beaten egg then roll it in the breadcrumbs.
7. Place a large pan over medium heat and heat the oil in it. Cook in it the shrimp patties until they become golden brown then serve them warm.
8. Enjoy.

Greek Style Turkish Chicken Kabobs

Prep Time: 15 mins
Total Time: 2 hr 27 min

Servings per Recipe: 4
Calories   539 kcal
Fat   32.5 g
Carbohydrates   8.4g
Protein   51.8 g
Cholesterol   186 mg
Sodium   1722 mg

Ingredients

- 1 C whole-milk Greek yogurt
- 2 tbsp freshly squeezed lemon juice, or more to taste
- 2 tbsp olive oil
- 2 tbsp ketchup
- 6 cloves garlic, minced
- 1 tbsp Aleppo red pepper flakes
- 1 tbsp kosher salt
- 1 1/2 tsp ground cumin
- 1 tsp freshly ground black pepper
- 1 tsp paprika
- 1/8 tsp ground cinnamon
- 2 1/2 lbs boneless, skinless chicken thighs, halved
- 4 long metal skewers

Directions

1. Get a mixing bowl: mix in it the yogurt, lemon juice, olive oil, ketchup, garlic, red pepper flakes, salt, cumin, black pepper, paprika, and cinnamon.
2. Stir in the chicken pieces into the mix. Put on a piece of plastic to cover them and place them in the fridge for 6 to 9 h.
3. Before you do anything preheat the grill and grease its grates. Grease the metal skewers.
4. Thread each chicken thigh into 2 skewers at the time horizontally. Cook the chicken kabobs for 4 to 5 min on each side then serve them.
5. Enjoy.

TILAPIA and Couscous Stew

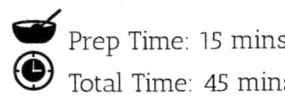

Prep Time: 15 mins
Total Time: 45 mins

Servings per Recipe: 4
Calories	456 kcal
Fat	12.4 g
Carbohydrates	53.4g
Protein	32.7 g
Cholesterol	42 mg
Sodium	762 mg

Ingredients
- 3 C water
- 1 1/2 C dry couscous
- 2 tbsp olive oil
- 1 small white onion, chopped
- 1 green bell pepper, chopped
- 2 cloves garlic, minced
- 1 C marinated artichoke hearts, liquid reserved
- 2 tsp capers, liquid reserved
- 12 small green olives
- 1 (14.5 oz) can chopped stewed tomatoes, drained
- 2 tbsp white wine (optional)
- 1 tbsp lemon juice
- 1 C water
- 2 tsp sumac powder
- 1 1/2 tsp crushed red pepper flakes
- 1 tsp dried basil
- 1 tsp cumin
- 1 tsp minced fresh ginger root
- Ground black pepper to taste
- 1 lb tilapia fillets, cut into chunks

Directions
1. Get a saucepan: place it over medium heat and fill it with 3 C of water. Cook them until the start boiling. Add the couscous and put on the lid.
2. Turn off the heat and let it rest for 6 min.
3. Place a large pan over medium heat. Heat the oil in it. Cook in it the onion and green pepper for 6 min. add the garlic and cook them for an extra 3 min.
4. Stir in the artichoke hearts with reserved liquid, capers with reserved liquid, and olives, tomatoes, wine, lemon juice, and 1 C water.
5. Add a pinch of salt and sumac powder, red pepper, basil, cumin, ginger, and pepper.
6. Cook them until they start boiling. Stir in the tilapia fish pieces and lower the heat. Cook the stew for 12 min.
7. Serve your tilapia stew with couscous.
8. Enjoy.

Yogurt Sauce with Poached Egg Breakfast

Prep Time: 15 mins
Total Time: 20 mins

Servings per Recipe: 2
Calories   442 kcal
Fat   29.4 g
Carbohydrates   16.2g
Protein   29.1 g
Cholesterol   600 mg
Sodium   1599 mg

Ingredients
- 3 cloves garlic, peeled and minced
- 1 1/2 C plain yogurt
- 1 pinch salt
- 1 quart water
- 1 tbsp vinegar
- 1 tsp salt
- 6 eggs
- 2 tbsp butter
- 1 tsp paprika

Directions
1. Get a small mixing bowl: whisk in it the garlic, yogurt and pinch of salt to make the sauce.
2. Place a large saucepan over high heat. Stir in it the water, vinegar and 1 tsp salt. Cook them until they start boiling.
3. Lower the heat and crack 1 egg at a time into the bubbling water leaving space between them. Let them cook until the white part is done then drain them.
4. Place the eggs on serving plate.
5. Place small pan over medium heat and heat the butter in it. Add to it the paprika and turn off the heat.
6. Drizzle the yogurt sauce over the mix and top it with the paprika butter mix. Serve it warm.
7. Enjoy.

CHEESY Chicken Casserole

Prep Time: 15 mins
Total Time: 55 mins

Servings per Recipe: 6
Calories   397 kcal
Fat   19.5 g
Carbohydrates   9.4g
Protein   43.7 g
Cholesterol   113 mg
Sodium   854 mg

Ingredients
2 tbsp olive oil, divided
1 1/2 lbs skinless, boneless chicken breast halves - cut into 1 inch cubes
1/2 (12 oz) jar roasted red bell peppers, drained
1 (14.5 oz) can diced tomatoes with juice
1 (6 oz) jar mushrooms, drained
1 onion, diced
1 tbsp minced garlic
Salt and pepper to taste
1 (16 oz) package shredded mozzarella cheese

Directions
1. Before you do anything preheat the oven to 350 f. grease a casserole dish and place it aside.
2. Place a large pan over medium heat and heat 1 tbsp of oil in it. Brown it in the chicken breasts on all sides.
3. Get a food processor: place the jarred peppers in it and process them until they become smooth.
4. Pour it into the casserole dish with the browned chicken, roasted red peppers, tomatoes, mushrooms, onion, and garlic, a pinch of salt and pepper.
5. Stir them well then top them with 1 tbsp of olive oil and mozzarella cheese. Place the casserole in the oven and cook it for 32 min. serve it warm.
6. Enjoy.

Warm Lentil Salad with Yogurt Sauce

Prep Time: 15 mins
Total Time: 1 h 30 mins

Servings per Recipe: 4
Calories	352 kcal
Fat	12.3 g
Carbohydrates	46.7 g
Protein	15.1 g
Cholesterol	3 mg
Sodium	239 mg

Ingredients

- 3 tbsp extra-virgin olive oil
- 1 onion, thinly sliced
- 1 clove garlic, minced
- 1 lb carrots cut into thin half-rounds
- 1 tbsp tomato paste
- 1/2 tsp ground chile pepper
- 1/4 tsp sea salt
- 3 C water
- 1 C lentil
- Salt and freshly ground black pepper to taste
- 1/4 C Greek yogurt

Directions

1. Place a large pan over medium heat. Add the oil in it and heat it. Sauté in it the onion for 8 min. stirs in the garlic and cook them for 3 min.
2. Add the carrots with tomato paste, ground chile pepper, and sea salt. Cook them for 3 min.
3. Place a large saucepan over medium heat. Stir in it the water with lentils and cook them until they start boiling. Put on the lid and lower the heat then cook it for 32 min.
4. Turn the heat to medium and add the cooked onion mix to the saucepan. Let them cook for 3 min. adjust the seasoning of the mix then serve it warm with some yogurt.
5. Enjoy.

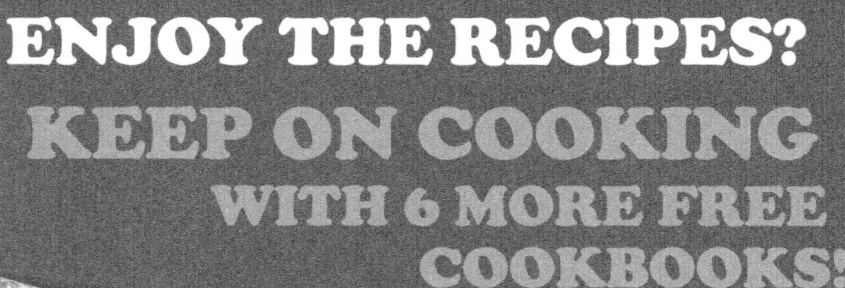

ENJOY THE RECIPES?
KEEP ON COOKING WITH 6 MORE FREE COOKBOOKS!

Visit our website and simply enter your email address to join the club and receive your 6 cookbooks.

http://booksumo.com/magnet

https://www.instagram.com/booksumopress/

https://www.facebook.com/booksumo/

Printed in Great Britain
by Amazon